Irresistible Italian

igloobooks

igloobooks

Published in 2018
by Igloo Books Ltd
Cottage Farm
Sywell
NN6 0BJ
www.igloobooks.com

The measurements used are approximate.

Food photography and recipe development:
© Stockfood, The Food Media Agency
Additional imagery: © iStock / Getty Images
Cover image: © iStock / Getty Images

STA002 0218
2 4 6 8 10 9 7 5 3 1
ISBN: 978-1-78810-176-9

Cover designed by Nicholas Gage
Interiors designed by Simon Parker
Edited by Jasmin Peppiatt

Printed and manufactured in China

Contents

Cook's Corner

Irresistible Italian

Meat and fish dishes

Parmesan stuffed tomatoes

SERVES: 4 | PREP TIME: 40 MINUTES | COOKING TIME: 30 MINUTES

INGREDIENTS

8 ripe beef tomatoes

salt

1 onion, peeled and finely chopped

2 cloves of garlic, finely chopped

1 tbsp olive oil

250 g / 9 oz / 1 cup minced beef

1 tbsp rosemary leaves, finely chopped

2 tbsp Parmesan, grated

METHOD

1. Using a teaspoon, hollow out the tomatoes, discarding the seeds.
2. Sprinkle the insides with a little salt and leave to drain upside down for 30 minutes.
3. Meanwhile, fry the onion and garlic in the oil.
4. Add the beef and rosemary, then turn up the heat and fry. Stir until the beef is cooked, then season. Stir in the Parmesan. Leave to cool.
5. Preheat the oven to 200°C (180°C fan) / 400F / gas 6.
6. Fill the tomatoes with the beef mixture and place in a roasting tin.
7. Drizzle with olive oil and bake in the oven for 30 minutes, or until the tomatoes are soft but retaining their shape. Serve hot or warm.

Beef carpaccio

SERVES: 4-6 | PREP TIME: 30 MINUTES | CHILLING TIME: 10 MINUTES

INGREDIENTS

250 g / 9 oz beef fillet, trimmed
handful rocket leaves
Parmesan shavings
1 tbsp capers, drained
extra virgin olive oil
½ lemon, juiced
salt and pepper

METHOD

1. Place the fillet in the freezer for 30 minutes to firm it up and make it easier to slice.
2. Slice the fillet as thinly as you possibly can with a razor-sharp knife. Place film over each slice to prevent discolouring and use it to stop the slices sticking together. You can keep them this way in the refrigerator until serving.
3. Thirty minutes before serving, remove the beef from the refrigerator and bring up to room temperature.
4. Decorate with the rocket, Parmesan and capers and drizzle over the oil and lemon. Season and serve.

Red pepper and ham tortilla

SERVES: 4 | PREP TIME: 10 MINUTES | COOKING TIME: 30 MINUTES

INGREDIENTS

60 ml / 2 fl. oz / ¼ cup olive oil
1 onion, thinly sliced
1 red pepper, quartered and thinly sliced
6 large eggs
1 tbsp flat-leaved parsley, chopped
4 slices ham, cooked
salt and pepper

METHOD

1. Heat half the oil in a non-stick pan over a mid-low heat. Fry the onion and red pepper with a pinch of salt for 15 minutes until soft and sweet.
2. Meanwhile, beat the eggs in a jug to break up the yolks. When the vegetables are ready, stir them into the eggs with the parsley and ham. Season.
3. Wipe out the frying pan with a piece of kitchen paper and add the rest of the oil. Pour in the egg mixture. Cook over a gentle heat for 6 minutes or until the egg has set around the outside.
4. Turn it out onto a plate, then slide it back into the pan and cook the other side for 4-6 minutes or until the egg is just set in the very centre. Leave to cool for 5 minutes then cut into wedges and serve.

Cod and vegetable minestrone

SERVES: 4 | PREP TIME: 20 MINUTES | COOKING TIME: 1 HOUR

INGREDIENTS

1 tbsp olive oil
70 g / 2 ¾ oz / ⅓ cup pancetta, chopped
1 carrot, peeled and finely chopped
2 celery stalks, finely chopped
2 potatoes, peeled and finely chopped
2 tomatoes, finely chopped
1 litre / 2 ½ pints / 5 cups chicken stock
60 g / 1 ½ oz / ¼ cup macaroni pasta
40 g / 1 oz frozen peas
1 courgette, finely chopped
400 g / 13 ½ oz / 1 ½ cups cod loin
extra virgin olive oil

METHOD

1. Heat the olive oil in a pan and cook the pancetta until the fat runs and it starts to turn golden.
2. Add the carrot and celery. Cook until softened.
3. Add the potatoes and tomatoes and cook for 2 minutes. Add the stock and simmer for 30 minutes until the vegetables are tender.
4. Once simmered, add the pasta and cook for a further 20 minutes.
5. Finish by adding the peas and courgette, then gently lower the fish into the soup and cook for another 10 minutes.
6. Ladle into bowls to serve, drizzled with oil.

Four seasons pizzas

SERVES: **3-4** | PREP TIME: **45 MINUTES** | COOKING TIME: **10 MINUTES**

INGREDIENTS

FOR THE DOUGH:

400 g / 13 ½ oz / 1 ½ cups strong white bread flour

100 g / 3 ½ oz / ½ cup fine ground semolina flour

½ tbsp salt

1 x 7 g sachet dried yeast

½ tbsp caster (superfine) sugar

350 ml / ½ pint / 1 ½ cups lukewarm water

FOR THE TOPPING, PER PIZZA:

6 tbsp bottled passata

2 slices ham

3 button mushrooms, thinly sliced

6 black olives, stoned

4 artichoke hearts, halved

80 g / 3 oz / ¼ cup mozzarella

extra virgin olive oil

METHOD

1. Pour the flours and salt into a bowl and make a well in the centre. Add the yeast and sugar, mix and leave for a few minutes. Once frothing, pour into the well.
2. Using a fork in a circular movement, slowly mix the flour into the water. When it starts coming together, use your hands to pat it into a ball.
3. Knead for 10 minutes, until it is elastic. Flour and cover with film. Leave to rest for 30 minutes.
4. Roll the pizzas out 30 minutes before cooking.
5. Preheat the oven to 250°C (230°C fan) / 500F / gas 9. Flour the surface, tear off a piece of dough and roll into a circle. Dust each circle with a little flour.
6. Spread the base of each with passata, then top each quarter with one of the ingredients and sprinkle the mozzarella cheese all over.
7. Place on a preheated baking sheet for 8-10 minutes until golden and crisp.

Chicken and cheese pizzas

SERVES: 6-8 | PREP TIME: 45 MINUTES | COOKING TIME: 8-10 MINUTES

INGREDIENTS

FOR THE DOUGH:

400 g / 13 ½ oz / 1 ½ cups strong white bread flour
100 g / 3 ½ oz / ½ cup fine ground semolina flour
½ tbsp salt
1 x 7 g sachet dried yeast
½ tbsp caster (superfine) sugar
350 ml / ½ pint / ⅓ cup lukewarm water

FOR THE TOPPING:

1 onion, sliced
2 tbsp butter
2 chicken breasts, skinned and chopped
1 tbsp mixed herbs
80 g / 3 oz / ⅓ cup Fourme d'Ambert cheese, per pizza
barbecue sauce, to serve

METHOD

1. Put the flour and salt into a bowl. Make a well
2. Add the yeast and sugar to the water and mix. Once frothing, pour into the well.
3. Bring in the flour from around the insides and mix into the water. When it starts to come together, pat it into a ball. Knead for 10 minutes, then flour the dough, cover with film and leave to rest for 30 minutes.
4. Cook the onion and butter in a pan until golden. Add the chicken and cook until the chicken is golden and tender.
5. Roll the pizzas out 30 minutes before you want to cook them.
6. Preheat the oven to 250°C (230°C fan) / 500F / gas 9. Flour the surface, tear off a piece of dough and roll into a circle about ½ cm thick.
7. Dust each one with flour and lay out on the surface.
8. Top with the chicken, onions, mixed herbs and sliced cheese. Place on a preheated baking sheet and place in the oven for 8-10 minutes until golden.
9. Serve immediately, drizzled with a little barbecue sauce, if desired.

Mini tomato anchovy tarts

SERVES: 6-8 | PREP TIME: 30 MINUTES | COOKING TIME: 12 MINUTES

INGREDIENTS

1 pack ready-rolled puff pastry
1 tbsp butter
1 onion, peeled and finely chopped
2 cloves of garlic, finely chopped
200 ml / 6 ½ fl. oz / ¾ cup passata
a small handful of oregano leaves
salt and pepper
1-2 ripe tomatoes, thickly sliced
8 anchovy fillets
8 black olives, stoned and halved

METHOD

1. Preheat the oven to 200°C (180°C fan) / 400F / gas 6.
2. Cut out pastry circles about 7 cm in diameter from the sheet. You should make between 6 and 8.
3. Place on a greased baking sheet and bake in the oven for 12 minutes until crisp and golden.
4. Once cooked, push the middle of each pastry circle down a little with a spoon to create a space for the filling.
5. Heat the butter in a pan and cook the onion and garlic until golden. Add the passata and oregano and heat briskly until reduced and thick.
6. Spoon into the middle of the pastry cases then top with a slice of fresh tomato. Place the anchovy and 2 olive halves on top and grill until bubbling. Leave to cool before eating.

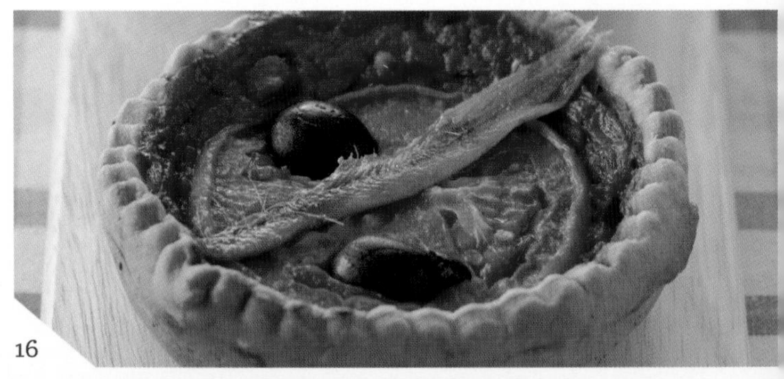

Veal piccata with courgettes

SERVES: 6 | PREP TIME: 15 MINUTES | COOKING TIME: 10 MINUTES

INGREDIENTS

4 courgettes

6 veal escalopes

60 g / 2 oz / ½ stick butter

1 lemon, juiced

250 g / 9 oz / 1 ⅔ cups mascarpone

salt and pepper

METHOD

1. Cut the courgette into strips. Steam for 5 minutes.
2. Place the veal escalopes between 2 sheets of cling film. Pound with a rolling pin until thin.
3. Heat the butter in a pan until foaming, then sear the escalopes on each side for 2 minutes. Add the lemon juice and increase the heat to reduce the liquid to a syrup. Pour over the escalopes.
4. Cut each escalope into 6 triangles. Thread 3 pieces onto a skewer, alternating with the courgettes. Repeat for the other skewers, then cover with foil to keep warm.
5. Add the mascarpone to the pan and deglaze. Pour in any resting juices from the veal. Pour this mixture over the veal skewers. Serve.

MEAT AND FISH

Bayonne ham crostini

SERVES: 6-8 | PREP TIME: 10 MINUTES | COOKING TIME: 3 HOURS 45 MINUTES

INGREDIENTS

4-5 ripe vine-grown plum tomatoes
1 ciabatta loaf, ready-to-bake
extra virgin olive oil
2 cloves of garlic, halved
300 g / 10 oz / 1 ¼ cups mozzarella
8 slices Bayonne ham
salt and pepper
basil

METHOD

1. Preheat the oven to 100°C (80°C fan) / 200F / gas 1.
2. Slice the tomatoes in half and scoop out the seeds. Salt the insides and leave to drain.
3. Place in a roasting tin, drizzle with a little oil and bake for 3 hours. Remove from the oven and set aside.
4. Heat the oven and bake the ciabatta loaf according to packet instructions. Leave to cool and firm up. Once cool, cut the loaf into 1.5cm thick slices.
5. Meanwhile, slice the tomatoes and sprinkle each one with a little salt.
6. Heat a griddle pan and lay the bread on the griddle until you achieve char marks across both sides. If you don't have a griddle, place the bread under the grill until lightly toasted.
7. Rub the toasted side with the cut garlic and drizzle with olive oil.
8. Lay half a slice of ham on each piece, then top with a little mozzarella.
9. Place a tomato half on top. Garnish with basil.

Chicken bake

SERVES: 4-6 | PREP TIME: 10 MINUTES | COOKING TIME: 45 MINUTES

INGREDIENTS

500 g / 1 lb 1 oz / 4 cups shaped pasta
2 tbsp olive oil
1 large onion, diced
2 cloves of garlic, finely chopped
400 g / 14 oz / 2 cups chicken breasts, cubed
1 tsp dried oregano
1 tbsp tomato purée
400 g / 14 oz / 2 cups canned chopped tomatoes
100 g / 3 ½ oz / ⅔ cup black olives, pitted
a small bunch of fresh basil, chopped
150 g / 5 ¼ oz / 1 ½ cups mozzarella cheese, grated

METHOD

1. Add the pasta to a pan of boiling water. Cook for 12-15 minutes then drain and set aside.
2. Heat the oil in a pan over a medium heat. Add the onion and fry for 4 minutes. Add the garlic and chicken then fry for 5 minutes. Add the oregano and tomato purée followed by the chopped tomatoes, olives and most of the basil. Season, cover and cook for 10 minutes.
3. Preheat the oven to 180°C (160°C fan) / 350F / gas 4.
4. Add the pasta and tomato sauce to an ovenproof dish and mix to combine. Cover with the grated cheese. Bake in the oven for 25 minutes.
5. Top with the reserved basil leaves and serve.

Seasoned beef carpaccio

SERVES: 4-6 | PREP TIME: 15 MINUTES | COOKING TIME: 30 MINUTES

INGREDIENTS

250 g / 9 oz piece of beef fillet

FOR THE DRESSING

2 egg yolks

100 ml / 3 ½ fl. oz / ⅖ cup olive oil

½ lemon, juiced

1 tbsp mustard

handful of rocket (arugula) leaves

Parmesan shavings

1 tbsp capers, drained

salt and pepper

METHOD

1. Place the fillet in the freezer for 30 minutes to firm it up and make it easier to slice.
2. Slice the fillet as thinly as you possibly can with a razor-sharp knife. Place film over each slice to prevent the slices sticking together. Keep them this way in the fridge until serving.
3. Around 30 minutes before serving, remove the beef from the refrigerator and bring up to room temperature.
4. To make the dressing, whizz the egg yolks in a blender, drizzling in the olive oil. Season with lemon juice and mustard.
5. Lay the beef on a plate then decorate with the rocket, Parmesan and capers. Drizzle over the dressing. Season and serve.

Prawn and chorizo paella

SERVES: 4 | PREP TIME: 5 MINUTES | COOKING TIME: 40 MINUTES

INGREDIENTS

1 litre / 1 pint 15 fl. oz / 4 cups chicken stock
1 pinch saffron
5 tbsp olive oil
1 onion, finely chopped
2 red peppers, diced
2 cloves of garlic, crushed
150 g / 5 ½ oz / 1 cup chorizo, halved and sliced
200 g / 7 oz / 1 cup paella rice
200 g / 7 oz / 1 cup raw prawns, peeled
1 small bunch flat-leaved parsley, chopped

METHOD

1. Heat the stock and saffron in a saucepan.
2. Heat the olive oil in a paella pan and gently fry the onion and peppers for 15 minutes. Add the garlic and chorizo and cook for 3 minutes.
3. Stir in the rice then let it toast for a minute. Pour in the hot stock and simmer without stirring for 10 minutes.
4. Distribute the prawns evenly into the liquid. Simmer for 5 more minutes.
5. Cover the pan with foil, turn off the heat and leave to stand for 5 minutes. Stir through the parsley and divide between four bowls.

Antipasti with polenta

SERVES: 4 | PREP TIME: 45-50 MINUTES | COOKING TIME: 50-60 MINUTES

INGREDIENTS

225 g / 9 oz / 1 cup polenta

1.7 litres / 3 pints / 6 cups water

2 red peppers

olive oil

salt and pepper

2 handfuls, black olives, stoned

4 slices Parma ham

jar of artichoke hearts

Parmesan

METHOD

1. Whisk the polenta in a pan of boiling water. Once it boils, cover with a lid slightly askew and turn the heat down.
2. When it begins to thicken, stir every 5 minutes. Cook for 45 minutes until it develops the consistency of mashed potato then season.
3. Oil a tray and tip the polenta out onto to it. Spread the polenta 2.5cm thick. Leave it to cool for 30 minutes and then cut into squares.
4. Preheat the oven to 200°C (180°C fan) / 400F / gas 7.
5. Cut the 'cheeks' off the peppers and roast in the oven with a little oil and seasoning until tender. Place in a plastic bag and leave for 20 minutes.
6. Peel the skins off the peppers when cool.
7. Cut the remaining ingredients into bite-sized pieces and use to top the polenta squares before serving.

Beef tartare

SERVES: 6 | PREP TIME: 20 MINUTES | COOKING TIME: 10 MINUTES

INGREDIENTS

500 g / 1 lb 2 oz pizza dough

900 g / 2 lb / 6 cups beef fillet, finely chopped

2 onions, peeled and very finely chopped

1 shallot, peeled and very finely chopped

a bunch of basil, chopped

5 tbsp olive oil

2 tbsp balsamic vinegar

salt and black pepper

1 tbsp Parmesan, grated

METHOD

1. Preheat the oven to 220°C (200°C fan) / 425F / gas 7.
2. Roll out the pizza dough on a floured surface to about 1mm thick, then cut into 12 small squares and place on greaseproof paper.
3. Bake in the oven for about 10 minutes. Once done, leave on a wire rack to cool.
4. Place the meat, onion, shallot, basil, olive oil and balsamic vinegar in a bowl and combine thoroughly, then season.
5. Spoon into 6 oiled circle moulds, pushing down gently.
6. Place 2 pizza squares on each plate, then top with the tartare. Garnish with Parmesan and a little more olive oil.

Lamb meatballs

SERVES: 4 | PREP TIME: 50 MINUTES | COOKING TIME: 15 MINUTES

INGREDIENTS

500 g / 1 lb 2 oz / 3 ⅓ cups minced lamb
1 onion, finely chopped
2 cloves of garlic, finely chopped
6 tbsp breadcrumbs
1 tbsp rosemary leaves, finely chopped
1 tbsp tomato purée
2 tbsp Parmesan, grated
½ lemon, zest grated
salt and pepper
2 tbsp olive oil
cooked rice, to serve

METHOD

1. Place the minced lamb in a large bowl until it reaches room temperature.
2. Add the rest of the ingredients and mix well with your hands to ensure even distribution.
3. Roll the mixture into small balls with your hands and place on a baking tray. Cover with cling film and refrigerate for 30 minutes.
4. Heat the olive oil in a large pan.
5. Add the meatballs in batches. Cook for about 6-8 minutes, on all sides, until golden and just cooked through.
6. Serve with cooked rice and a sauce of your choice.

Leek and trout bake

SERVES: 4 | PREP TIME: 10 MINUTES | COOKING TIME: 20-25 MINUTES

INGREDIENTS

12 lasagne sheets

4 leeks, trimmed and finely sliced

40 g / 1 ½ oz butter

200 g / 6 ½ oz / ¾ cup smoked trout fillets

300 ml / 10 fl oz / 1 ¼ cups crème fraîche

½ bunch dill, finely chopped

zest and juice of ½ lemon

METHOD

1. Cook the pasta in boiling salted water according to packet instructions.
2. Drain, brush over a little oil and keep warm.
3. Cook the leeks very gently in the butter with a sprinkling of salt until very soft and sweet.
4. Meanwhile flake the trout fillets into a bowl, removing any bones.
5. Gently mix with the crème fraîche, dill, lemon zest and a little juice. Season well.
6. Layer the lasagne sheets onto plates, 3 per serving. Spoon over the trout and crème fraîche filling, then top with leeks, then another layer of pasta and repeat.
7. Serve drizzled with extra virgin olive oil.

Smoked chicken risotto

SERVES: 4 | PREP TIME: 10-15 MINUTES | COOKING TIME: 40-50 MINUTES

INGREDIENTS

2 tbsp coconut oil
1 shallot, finely chopped
2 cloves of garlic, minced
200 g / 7 oz / 1 cup short-grain rice
110 ml / 4 fl. oz / ½ cup dry white wine
1 l / 1 pint 16 fl oz / 4 cups hot chicken stock
2 chicken breasts, pre-cooked and cubed
75 g / 2 ½ oz / ½ cup frozen peas

METHOD

1. Heat the coconut oil in a large, shallow saucepan over a medium heat.
2. Add the shallot, garlic and a little salt, sweating for 4–5 minutes until fully softened.
3. Add the rice and cook for 2–3 minutes, stirring frequently. Then add the dry white wine and let it reduce by half.
4. Pour the chicken stock into the rice then stir every minute or so for 30-35 minutes until the rice fully absorbs the liquid. Around 25 minutes into this cooking time, add the frozen peas, which will defrost and cook in the remaining 5-10 minutes.
5. Once the rice is plump and tender, stir through the chicken, then season to taste.
6. Spoon into bowls and serve.

Seafood minestrone

SERVES: 4 | PREP TIME: 10 MINUTES | COOKING TIME: 35-45 MINUTES

INGREDIENTS

1 tbsp olive oil
1 onion, peeled and finely chopped
1 carrot, peeled and finely chopped
1 celery stalk, peeled and chopped
2 tomatoes, finely chopped
1 L / 2 pints / 4 ¼ cups chicken stock
50 g / 1 ½ oz / ⅕ cup macaroni pasta
750 g / 1 ¼ lb / 3 cups mixed raw seafood, such as prawns, scallops and squid
1 bunch parsley, chopped
½ lemon

METHOD

1. Heat the olive oil in a pan and sweat the onion, carrot and celery without colouring for 5 minutes.
2. Add the tomatoes and cook for a further 2 minutes. Pour over the stock, bring to a simmer and add the pasta.
3. Cook for about 20 minutes until the pasta is tender. Add the seafood and poach in the soup until the prawns turn pink, the scallops opaque and the mussels open. Discard any that remain closed.
4. Scatter over the parsley and adjust the seasoning as desired.

Ham and tomato salad

SERVES: 4 | PREP TIME: 15 MINUTES

INGREDIENTS

4 ripe vine-grown tomatoes

2 buffalo mozzarella balls

salt and pepper

extra virgin olive oil

8 slices Parma ham

basil

METHOD

1. Slice the tomatoes thickly, drizzle with oil and a little salt and leave to stand for 10 minutes.
2. Tear the mozzarella into pieces.
3. Arrange the tomatoes and mozzarella in an alternating pattern on a serving platter, drizzling over the juices from the tomatoes.
4. Lay the ham alongside.
5. Scatter over torn basil leaves and drizzle with more oil and a little pepper.

Scallop fricassée

SERVES: 4 | PREP TIME: 10 MINUTES | COOKING TIME: 40 MINUTES

INGREDIENTS

FOR THE POLENTA:
200 g / 7 oz / 1 cup polenta
1.5 l / 2 pints 12 fl. oz / 6 cups water
110 g / 4 oz / 1 stick butter
110 g / 4 oz / 1 cup Parmesan, grated

FOR THE SCALLOPS:
40 g / 1 ½ oz butter
8 scallops, cleaned
75 g / 3 oz / 1 cup girolle mushrooms, brushed clean
1 clove of garlic, finely chopped
½ lemon, juiced
¼ bunch parsley, chopped

METHOD

1. Whisk the polenta into a pan of boiling water. As soon as it begins to boil, cover loosely and turn the heat down to minimum.
2. Once it thickens, stir. Cook for 30 minutes. Add water to get the consistency of whipped cream.
3. Take off the heat, stir in the butter and Parmesan then season. Set aside and keep warm.
4. Heat the butter in a pan. Season the scallops. When the butter is foaming, place in the pan.
5. Add the mushrooms and garlic. Cook for 4 minutes, turning the scallops halfway through.
6. Remove the scallops from the pan when opaque. Season the mushrooms. Add the lemon and parsley. Spoon the warm polenta onto a plate. Top with the mushrooms. Arrange the scallops on top.

Seafood pizzas

SERVES: 2-3 | PREP TIME: 45 MINUTES | COOKING TIME: 8-10 MINUTES

INGREDIENTS

FOR THE DOUGH:

400 g / 13 ½ oz / 1 ½ cups strong white bread flour
100 g / 3 ½ oz / ½ cup fine ground semolina flour
½ tbsp salt
1 x 7 g sachet dried yeast
½ tbsp caster (superfine) sugar
approx. 350 ml / ½ pint / ⅓ cup lukewarm water

FOR THE TOPPING:

10 tbsp passata
handful black olives, stoned
200 g / 6 ½ oz / ¾ cup raw prawns, shelled
1 green chilli, finely sliced
1 scallop per pizza

METHOD

1. Pour the flours and salt into a bowl and make a well in the centre. Add the yeast and sugar to the water and mix. When frothing, pour into the well.
2. Bring in the flour from around the insides. Mix into the water. When it starts coming together, pat it into a ball. Knead for 10 minutes. Then, flour the dough. Cover with film. Leave for 30 minutes.
3. Preheat the oven to 250°C (230°C fan) / 500F / gas 9.
4. Flour the surface, tear off a piece of dough and roll into a circle about 0.5 cm thick. Dust each one with flour and lay out on the surface.
5. Spread 1 tablespoon of passata on each pizza. Top each one with the olives, prawns and chilli.
6. Slice the scallops in half and place on the pizza. Place on a preheated baking sheet for 10 minutes until golden.

Rustic tomato soup

SERVES: 4 | PREP TIME: 15 MINUTES | COOKING TIME: 30-35 MINUTES

INGREDIENTS

2 tbsp olive oil
1 onion, peeled and chopped
1 carrot, peeled and finely chopped
1 celery stalk, finely chopped
2 cloves of garlic, chopped
1 courgette, finely chopped
2 potatoes, peeled and finely chopped
2 slices Parma ham, chopped
400 g / 14 oz / 2 cups canned chopped tomatoes
1 dried red chilli (chili), chopped
1 l / 1 pint 16 fl. oz / 4 cups chicken stock
salt and pepper
extra virgin olive oil

METHOD

1. Heat the oil in a pan and sweat the onion, carrot and celery without colouring. Add the garlic and cook for 2 minutes until soft.
2. Add the courgettes and potatoes, stir well and then leave to soften for 5-10 minutes, then add the ham.
3. Pour in the tomatoes, crumble in a little of the chilli, then stir in the stock.
4. Bring to a simmer and leave to cook for around 20 minutes until the vegetables are tender and cooked through.
5. Taste and adjust the seasoning if necessary, adding chilli if desired.
6. Roughly mash the vegetables with a potato masher or pulse in a liquidizer if a smoother consistency is required.
7. Serve drizzled with olive oil.

Tuna and cannellini bean salad

SERVES: 1 | PREP TIME: 15 MINUTES

INGREDIENTS

200 g / 7 oz / 1 cup canned cannellini beans, drained

1 shallot, finely diced

1 clove garlic, minced

1 lemon, juiced

1 tbsp extra virgin olive oil

handful of fresh basil, chopped

½ red onion, sliced

160 g / 5 ½ oz / ⅔ cup canned tuna

sea salt and black pepper

METHOD

1. Add the beans, shallot, garlic, lemon juice, oil and basil to a bowl.
2. Mix well and season to taste.
3. Add the onion and drained tuna to the bean mixture and quickly toss together.
4. Spoon into a serving bowl and garnish with a sprig of fresh basil.
5. Serve with freshly baked bread for a simple and hearty meal.

Prawns alla busara

SERVES: 2 | PREP TIME: 15 MINUTES | COOKING TIME: 20 MINUTES

INGREDIENTS

75 ml / 2 ½ fl. oz / ⅓ cup olive oil
2 shallots, diced
2 cloves garlic, chopped
1 red chilli (chili), deseeded and sliced
1 tbsp tomato paste
600 g / 1 lb 3 oz raw whole king prawns
200 ml / 7 fl. oz / ¾ cup white wine
handful of flat-leaved parsley, chopped
side salad, to serve

METHOD

1. Heat two-thirds of the oil in a large heavy bottomed pan over a medium heat. Add the shallots, garlic and chilli and fry for 2-3 minutes until sizzling.
2. Stir in the tomato paste and a pinch of salt, then continue to fry for a further minute, stirring continuously.
3. Add the prawns to the pan and fry for a minute until they begin to change colour. Pour in the wine and allow to bubble and reduce for 12-15 minutes until the prawns are cooked and the sauce has thickened.
4. Add the parsley and toss through to ensure all the prawns are coated in the sauce.
5. Serve with a simple side salad.

Artichoke pancetta risotto

SERVES: 2 | PREP TIME: 10 MINUTES | COOKING TIME: 40 MINUTES

INGREDIENTS

1 onion, diced

2 cloves garlic, minced

2 tbsp butter

250 g / 9 oz / 1 ¼ cup Arborio risotto rice

200 ml / 7 fl. oz / ¾ cup white wine

500 ml / 17 fl. oz / 2 cups chicken stock, warm

50 g / 1 ¾ oz Parmesan cheese, grated

200 g / 7 oz / 1 cup diced pancetta

200 g / 7 oz / 1 cup grilled artichoke hearts, sliced

sea salt and black pepper

extra virgin olive oil, to serve

METHOD

1. Heat some oil in a heavy bottomed lidded pan over a medium heat. Add the onion and fry for 3-4 minutes. Add the garlic and fry for 1 more minute.
2. Add half the butter and the rice to the pan. Stir, then turn the heat up and add the wine. Allow to bubble for 5 minutes or until the liquid has reduced by half, then turn the heat down to a medium heat.
3. Gradually add the stock to the rice, placing the lid on the pan after each addition. It will be ready when the rice is cooked but still has a slight bite Then, stir through the remaining butter and grated cheese once the risotto is cooked.
4. Fry the pancetta in a hot pan until crisp. To serve, spoon the risotto onto serving plates. Top with the artichokes and pancetta then drizzle with oil.

Veal Milanese

SERVES: 2 | PREP TIME: 15 MINUTES | COOKING TIME: 15 MINUTES

INGREDIENTS

2 veal escalopes, approx. 150 g / 5 ¼ oz each

2 free-range eggs

2 tbsp plain (all-purpose) flour

200 g / 7 oz / 1 ⅓ cups panko breadcrumbs, lightly crushed

25 g / 1 oz butter

2 tbsp olive oil

sea salt and freshly ground black pepper

pasta, to serve

METHOD

1. Start by flattening out the veal by placing it between 2 sheets of cling film and hitting it with a rolling pin. Be careful to not break the meat.
2. Beat the eggs and place into a bowl, then place the flour onto a plate and season with salt and pepper. Place the breadcrumbs on a separate plate.
3. Take the veal. Dip it first into the flour, then the egg and finally the breadcrumbs. Ensure that the meat is coated and shake off any excess.
4. Heat the butter and oil in a frying pan over a mid- high heat. Once hot, add the breaded veal and fry for around 5-8 minutes on each side.
5. Remove from the pan and place onto kitchen paper to drain. Serve with some simple pasta drizzled with olive oil.

Sausage, olive and mozzarella pizza

SERVES: 2 | PREP TIME: 1 HOUR 15 MINUTES | COOKING TIME: 10 MINUTES

INGREDIENTS

FOR THE DOUGH:

500 g / 1 lb 1 oz / 3 ⅓ cups white bread flour

1 tsp salt

1 tsp active dry yeast

1 tsp caster (superfine) sugar

300 ml / 10 ½ fl. oz / 1 ¼ cup water, lukewarm

25 ml extra virgin olive oil

FOR THE TOPPING:

100 g / 3 ½ oz / ½ cup passata

2 tsp dried oregano

75 g / 2 ½ oz pepperoni, sliced

100 g / 3 ½ oz / 1 cup mozzarella, grated

50 g / 1 ¾ oz / ⅓ cup black olives

125 g / 4 ¼ oz / 1 ¼ cup buffalo mozzarella, sliced

handful of basil leaves

50 g / 1 ¾ oz rocket (arugula)

handful of chopped cherry tomatoes

METHOD

1. Mix the flour and salt in a large mixing bowl. Combine the yeast, sugar, water and oil in a jug and leave for a few minutes until frothy.
2. Make a well in the centre of the flour and pour in the wet ingredients. Mix together with a fork until the dough starts to form. Knead until you have a soft, springy dough.
3. Place into a floured bowl and cover with a damp cloth and leave in a warm place until doubled in size. This should take 1 hour.
4. When risen, knock back the dough and separate into two balls. Roll out on a floured surface to the desired shape and leave for a further 10-15 minutes.
5. Preheat the oven to 240°C (220°C fan) / 475F / gas 9.
6. Spread the passata onto the pizza bases and top with the oregano, pepperoni, grated mozzarella and olives. Cook in the hot oven for 10-12 minutes until the cheese has melted.
7. Top the cooked pizza with the buffalo mozzarella, basil, rocket and tomatoes. Season before serving.

Pepperoni pizza

SERVES: 2 | PREP TIME: 1 HOUR 30 MINUTES | COOKING TIME: 12 MINUTES

INGREDIENTS

FOR THE DOUGH:

500 g / 1 lb 1 oz / 3 ⅓ cup white bread flour
1 tsp salt
1 tsp active dry yeast
1 tsp caster (superfine) sugar
300 ml / 10 ½ fl. oz / 1 ¼ cup water, lukewarm
2 tbsp extra virgin olive oil

FOR THE TOPPING:

100 g / 3 ½ oz / ½ cup passata
2 tsp dried oregano
1 tsp garlic granules
200 g / 7 oz / 1 cup mozzarella, sliced
1 large tomato, sliced
50 g / 1 ¾ oz pepperoni slices
25 g / 1 oz black olives, sliced
½ red pepper, thinly sliced
handful of basil leaves
salt and freshly ground black pepper

METHOD

1. Mix the flour and salt in a mixing bowl. Combine the yeast, sugar, water and oil in a jug and leave for a few minutes until frothy.
2. Make a well in the centre of the flour and pour in the wet ingredients. Mix together with a fork until the dough starts to form. Knead until you have a soft, springy dough.
3. Place into a floured bowl and cover with a damp cloth. Leave in a warm place to double in size. This should take roughly an hour.
4. When risen, knock back the dough and separate into two balls. Roll out on a floured surface to the desired shape and leave for a further 10-15 minutes.
5. Preheat the oven to 240°C (220°C fan) / 475F / gas 9.
6. Spread the passata over the prepared bases and then top with the remaining ingredients apart from the basil.
7. Place into the hot oven and cook for 10-12 minutes. The base should be crisp and cheese melted when ready. Remove and sprinkle over the basil leaves.

Squash and pancetta tart

SERVES: 1 | PREP TIME: 15 MINUTES | COOKING TIME: 45 MINUTES

INGREDIENTS

1 butternut squash
2 tbsp olive oil
1 onion, diced
1 clove of garlic, minced
200 g / 7 oz / 1 cup cubetti di pancetta
2 tsp dried oregano
500 g / 1 lb 1 oz block puff pasty
50 g / 1 ¾ oz / ½ cup chopped walnuts
sea salt and freshly ground black pepper
extra virgin olive oil, to drizzle

METHOD

1. Preheat the oven to 220°C (200°C fan) / 425F / gas 7.
2. Peel and deseed the squash and cut into small cubes.
3. Heat the oil in a non-stick pan over a medium heat. Add the onion and cook for 6-8 minutes until soft. Add the garlic. Fry for 1 more minute.
4. Add the pancetta to the pan. Fry for 4 minutes until starting to colour. Add the cubed squash and oregano to the pan. Toss to coat with the oil and fat from the pancetta. Fry for another 8 minutes until the squash starts to soften.
5. Roll out the pastry on a floured surface. Shape into a large round pizza shape and transfer to a baking tray.
6. Place the squash and pancetta mix onto the pastry leaving a 4 cm ring around the edge. Sprinkle over the chopped nuts and season with sea salt and ground black pepper.
7. Bake in the oven for 30 minutes or until the pastry has risen and the centre is cooked. Remove from the oven and drizzle with extra virgin oil before serving.

Prawn and porcini salad

SERVES: 1 | PREP TIME: 15 MINUTES | COOKING TIME: 15 MINUTES

INGREDIENTS

2 tbsp olive oil
50 g / 1 ¾ oz porcini mushrooms, sliced
1 tsp dried oregano
100 g / 3 ½ oz / ½ cup raw prawns, tails on
1 lemon, juice
75 g / 2 ½ oz mixed salad leaves
handful of cherry tomatoes, halved

METHOD

1. Heat half the oil in a frying pan over a mid-high heat. Once hot, add the mushrooms and cook for 8 minutes until starting to crisp. Sprinkle with the oregano.
2. Add the prawns to the pan. Cook for a further 5 minutes until they have changed colour and feel firm. Squeeze over the lemon juice and season then remove from the heat.
3. Mix the salad leaves and tomatoes in a bowl and coat with the remaining oil and season.
4. Place the salad onto a serving plate and top with the prawns and mushrooms.

Pork in Marsala sauce

SERVES: 2 | PREP TIME: 10 MINUTES | COOKING TIME: 25 MINUTES

INGREDIENTS

2 tbsp olive oil
300 g / 10 ½ oz pork medallions
2 shallots, diced
1 clove of garlic, minced
150 g / 5 ¼ oz / 1 cup chestnut mushrooms, sliced
75 ml / 2 ½ fl. oz / ⅓ cup Marsala
100 ml / 3 ½ fl. oz / ½ cup chicken stock
100 ml / 3 ½ fl. oz / ½ cup double (heavy) cream
2 tbsp tarragon leaves, chopped
100 g / 3 ½ oz / ¾ cup gemelli pasta
sea salt and ground black pepper
parsley, to garnish
cherry tomatoes, to garnish

METHOD

1. In a large sauté pan, heat the oil over a mid-high heat. Once hot, cook the pork medallions for 2-3 minutes on each side and remove to a clean plate and cover with foil.
2. Turn the heat down a little. Add the shallots and garlic. Fry for 3 minutes. Add the mushrooms. Fry for 8 minutes, until the edges start to colour.
3. Return the pork to the pan. Turn the heat back up. Add the Marsala wine to the pan. Allow to bubble until the liquid reduces by half. Turn the heat back down to medium. Add the stock, cream and tarragon. Stir, then simmer for 8 minutes.
4. Cook the pasta as per the packet instructions. Drain the pasta and add to the pan with the pork. Mix to combine, and serve with parsley and tomatoes as a garnish, if desired.

Italian meatballs

SERVES: 4 | PREP TIME: 30 MINUTES | COOKING TIME: 20 MINUTES

INGREDIENTS

FOR THE MEATBALLS:

300 g / 10 ½ oz / 1 ½ cups beef mince
200 g / 7 oz / 1 cup pork mince
1 egg, beaten
50 g / 1 ¾ oz / ½ cup Parmesan cheese, finely grated
1 clove of garlic, minced
1 tsp dried oregano
1 tsp fennel seeds, crushed
salt and freshly ground black pepper

FOR THE SAUCE:

2 tbsp olive oil
1 onion, diced
1 red pepper, diced
1 clove of garlic, minced
125 ml / 4 ½ fl. oz / ½ cup red wine
400 g / 14 oz / 2 cups canned plum tomatoes
handful of basil leaves, chopped
handful of flat-leaf parsley, to garnish
crusty bread, to serve

METHOD

1. Using your hands, combine all of the meatball ingredients in a mixing bowl.
2. Form the meatball mixture into balls around the size of a golf ball. Place onto a plate and then refrigerate for 20 minutes before cooking.
3. While the meatballs are chilling, heat half the oil in a saucepan over a medium heat. Add the onion and pepper and cook for 5 minutes until softened. Add the garlic and cook for a further minute.
4. Turn up the heat and add the wine. Allow to reduce by around half before turning the heat back down and adding the tomatoes. Cook for 8-10 minute or until the tomatoes start to break down.
5. Add the basil leaves and season well, then blend using a hand blender, according to the manufacturer's instructions.
6. Heat the remaining oil in a large frying pan and cook the meatballs for around 8-10 minutes until crisp. You may have to do this in batches.
7. Garnish with parsley, then serve the meatballs with the tomato sauce and crusty bread.

Seafood fagioli soup

SERVES: 2 | PREP TIME: 10 MINUTES | COOKING TIME: 30 MINUTES

INGREDIENTS

1 tbsp olive oil
1 onion, diced
2 cloves of garlic, crushed
2 sticks celery, diced
80 g / 2 ¾ oz / ⅔ cup cubetti di pancetta
1 tsp sweet paprika
1 tbsp tomato purée
400 g / 14 oz / 2 cups canned chopped tomatoes
400 g / 14 oz / 2 cups canned cannellini beans, drained
150 g / 5 ¼ oz / ¾ cup squid rings
200 g / 7 oz / 1 cup raw king prawns
150 g / 5 ¼ oz / ¾ cup spaghetti, broken into smaller pieces
sprig of basil, to garnish

METHOD

1. Heat the oil in a large casserole pot over a medium heat. Add the onion, garlic, celery and pancetta and cook for 10 minutes, stirring regularly, until golden in colour.
2. Add the paprika and tomato purée and cook for a further minute before adding the tomatoes. Cover and allow to simmer for 15 minutes.
3. Add the beans to the soup along with the squid and prawns. Cook for a further 10-15 minutes until the prawns are pink and firm.
4. At the same time, bring a pan of salted water to the boil. Once boiling add the spaghetti and cook for 12-15 minutes until cooked. Add the cooked spaghetti to the soup along with some of the pasta water if the soup has become too thick.
5. Serve in bowls with a basil sprig as a garnish.

Meatballs al forno

SERVES: 4 | PREP TIME: 15 MINUTES | COOKING TIME: 45 MINUTES

INGREDIENTS

200 g / 7 oz / 1 cup beef mince
200 g / 7 oz / 1 cup pork mince
1 egg, beaten
50 g / 1 ¾ oz / ½ cup Parmesan cheese, finely grated
1 tsp dried oregano
1 lemon, zest only
25 g / 1 oz sun-dried tomatoes, chopped
salt and freshly ground black pepper
2 tbsp olive oil
1 onion, diced
1 red pepper, diced
2 cloves of garlic, minced
2 anchovy fillets
1 tsp chilli (chili) flakes
125 ml / 4 ½ fl. oz / ½ cup red wine
400 g / 14 oz / 2 cups canned plum tomatoes
small bunch of basil leaves, chopped
160 g / 5 ½ oz / 1 ½ cup mozzarella cheese, grated

METHOD

1. Preheat the oven to 200°C (180°C fan) / 400F / gas 6.
2. Place the first seven ingredients in a large mixing bowl. Using your hands mix all the ingredients to fully combine. Form into tennis ball sized meatballs and set aside.
3. Heat half the oil in a saucepan over a medium heat. Add the onion and pepper and cook for 5 minutes until softened. Add the garlic, anchovies and chilli and cook for a further minute.
4. Turn up the heat and add the wine. Allow to reduce by around half before turning the heat back down and adding the tomatoes and juice. Cook for 8-10 minutes or until the tomatoes start to break down. Add half the basil and season.
5. Heat the remaining oil in a large frying pan and cook the meatballs for around 8-10 minutes until crisp and browned.
6. Transfer the meatballs to an ovenproof dish and pour over the sauce. Top with the grated mozzarella cheese, remaining basil and season.
7. Bake in the oven for 20 minutes until the cheese has melted and serve.

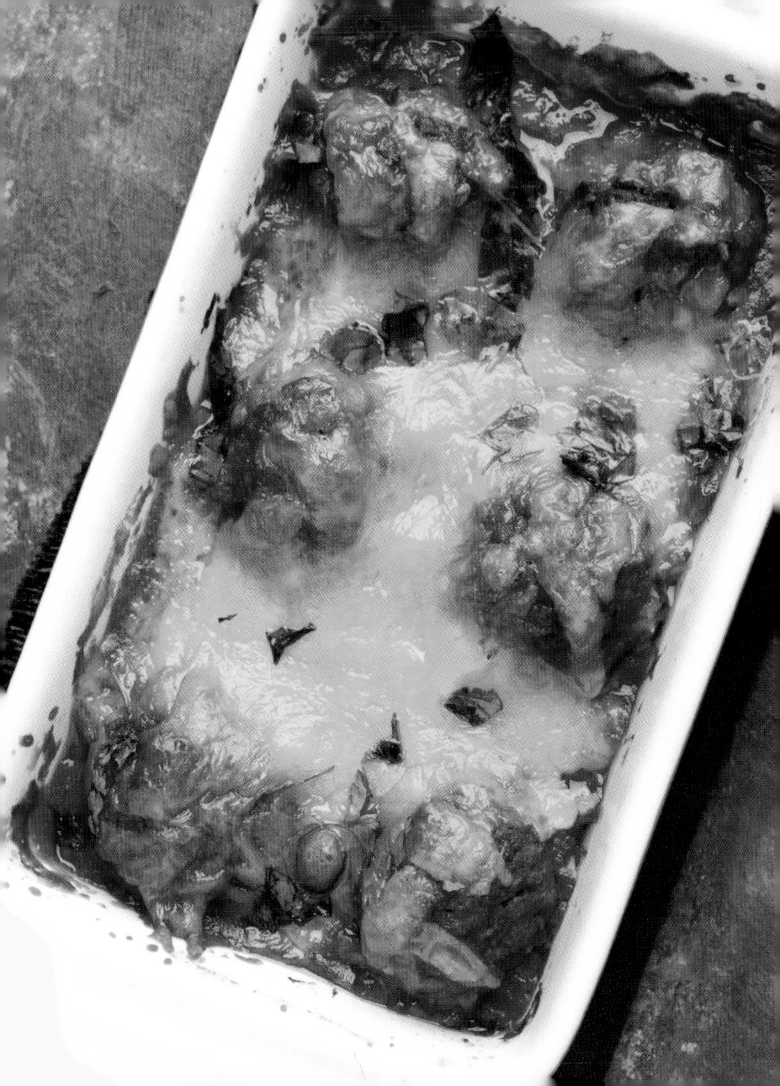

Turkey meatballs all'arrabbiata

SERVES: 4 | PREP TIME: 20 MINUTES | COOKING TIME: 30 MINUTES

INGREDIENTS

800 g / 1 lb 7 oz / 4 cups canned chopped tomatoes
25 ml / 1 fl. oz olive oil
2 garlic cloves, minced
1 tsp chilli (chili) flakes
handful of fresh basil, chopped
1 tsp dried oregano
400 g / 14 oz / 2 cups lean turkey mince
100 g / 3 ½ oz / ½ cup pork mince
handful of flat-leaved parsley, chopped
1 tsp garlic granules
50 g / 1 ¾ oz / ½ cup Parmesan cheese, grated
1 egg, beaten
sea salt and cracked black pepper

METHOD

1. Place the tomatoes and olive oil into a wide deep pan and bring to a steady simmer.
2. Add the garlic, chilli, basil and oregano and season to taste. Continue to simmer until the sauce begins to thicken.
3. Place the turkey, pork, parsley, garlic granules, cheese and egg into a bowl and bring together with your hands. Season with salt and black pepper.
4. Wet your hands, and form meatballs roughly the size of the palm of your hand.
5. Place the meatballs into the sauce and cook for 12-15 minutes, ensuring that the meatballs are completely cooked through.
6. Season to taste and scatter with chopped herbs then serve with crusty bread or pasta.

Cold fusilli salad

SERVES: 2 | PREP TIME: 10 MINUTES | COOKING TIME: 15 MINUTES

INGREDIENTS

100 g / 3 ½ oz / 1 cup fusilli
1 red pepper, sliced
½ cucumber, sliced
50 g / 1 ¾ oz / ⅓ cup black olives, pitted
100 g / 3 ½ oz / ½ cup roast ham, diced
2 tbsp extra virgin olive oil
sea salt and black pepper

METHOD

1. Cook the fusilli in a pan of salted water as per the packet instructions.
2. Drain well and leave to cool.
3. Combine the cooled pasta with the remaining ingredients in a mixing bowl.
4. Toss to coat the ingredients with the oil and seasoning.
5. Place into serving bowls or into an air tight container for food on the go.

Cook's Corner

Irresistible Italian

Vegetable and cheese dishes

Vegetable minestrone

SERVES: 4 | PREP TIME: 20 MINUTES | COOKING TIME: 45 MINUTES

INGREDIENTS

2 tbsp olive oil
1 onion, diced
2 celery sticks, chopped
2 carrots, sliced
2 cloves of garlic, chopped
1 courgette (zucchini), sliced
1 red pepper, deseeded and chopped
400 g / 14 oz / 2 cups canned chopped tomatoes
1 ltr / 33 ¾ fl. oz / 4 cups chicken or vegetable stock
150 g / 5 ¼ oz / ¾ cup ditalini pasta or similar small shape
200 g / 7 oz / 1 ⅓ cup garden peas, frozen
handful of basil leaves, chopped
50 g / 1 ¾ oz / ½ cup Parmesan cheese, grated
sea salt and freshly ground black pepper

METHOD

1. Heat the oil in a large saucepan with a lid over a medium heat. Add the onion, celery and carrot and cook for 8-10 minutes until softened.
2. Add the garlic, courgette and pepper to the pan and continue to cook for 2-3 more minutes.
3. Add the chopped tomatoes followed by the chicken stock. Bring to the boil before placing the lid on top and reducing the heat to a simmer. Cook for 10-15 minutes until the vegetables have softened.
4. Add the pasta to the pan and cook for a further 12-15 minutes until the pasta is cooked. Add the peas for the last 3-5 minutes to cook. Check the seasoning to taste and add more water if the soup is too thick.
5. To serve, ladle the soup into bowls and top with chopped basil, grated Parmesan and a drizzle of extra virgin olive oil.

Peperonata

SERVES: 4 | PREP TIME: 15 MINUTES | COOKING TIME: 45 MINUTES

INGREDIENTS

80 ml / 2 ¾ fl. oz / ⅓ cup olive oil
2 onions, sliced
4 mixed peppers, deseeded and sliced lengthways
200 g / 7 oz / 1 cup canned plum tomatoes, chopped
salt and cracked black pepper
crusty bread, to serve

METHOD

1. Heat the oil in a heavy bottomed pan over a medium heat. Add the onions with a pinch of salt and allow to slow soften but not colour.
2. Add the sliced peppers to the pan and mix into the onions.
3. Add the chopped plum tomatoes and mix through. Cover and cook on a low simmer for 35-40 minutes until the mixture is soft and rich.
4. Season with salt and black pepper.
5. Serve in bowl with crusty bread to soak up the juices.

Rustic vegetable broth

SERVES: 4 | PREP TIME: 15 MINUTES | COOKING TIME: 30 MINUTES

INGREDIENTS

1 tbsp olive oil
2 leeks, sliced
2 carrots, diced
2 courgettes (zucchinis), diced
1 ltr / 33 ¾ fl. oz / 4 cups vegetable stock
200 g / 7 oz / 1 ⅓ cup potatoes, peeled and sliced
200 g / 7 oz / 1 ⅓ cup peas, frozen
handful of sage leaves
1 tsp chilli (chili) flakes
salt and freshly ground black pepper

METHOD

1. Heat the oil in a large pan with a lid over a medium heat. Add the leeks, carrots and courgettes and fry for 6-8 minutes until starting to soften but not colour.
2. Pour in the vegetable stock, bring to the boil before covering and lowering to a simmer.
3. After 10 minutes add the potatoes to the pot, followed by the peas and sage leaves 10 minutes later. Season with salt and black pepper and cook for a further 5 -10 minutes.
4. The broth will be ready once the potatoes are soft but firm enough not to break easily.
5. Ladle into serving bowls and sprinkle with chilli flakes to serve.

Italian style quiche

SERVES: 1 | PREP TIME: 10 MINUTES | COOKING TIME: 30 MINUTES

INGREDIENTS

4 free-range eggs

350 g / 12 ⅓ oz / 2 ½ cups ricotta

50 g / 1 ¾ oz / ½ cup Parmesan, grated

500 g / 1 lb 1 oz block puff pastry

1 yellow pepper, deseeded and sliced

100 g / 3 ½ oz / ½ cup cherry tomatoes, halved

salt and ground black pepper

METHOD

1. Preheat the oven to 220°C (200°C fan) / 425F / gas 7 and grease and line a baking tray.
2. Mix the eggs, ricotta and Parmesan and whisk together until thick. Season.
3. Roll out the pastry and shape to a 40cm circle, transfer to the baking tray.
4. Spread the egg mixture into the centre of the pastry leaving a 5 cm gap around the edge. Fold the edges up around the egg mixture to create the sides of the quiche.
5. Place the peppers and tomatoes into the egg mixture. Bake in the oven for 30 minutes or until the centre of the quiche has set.
6. Serve either warm or cold with a side salad.

Mushroom risotto

SERVES: 2 | PREP TIME: 15 MINUTES | COOKING TIME: 30 MINUTES

INGREDIENTS

2 tbsp oil
1 onion, diced
2 cloves garlic, minced
2 tbsp butter
300 g / 10 ½ oz / 1 ½ cups Arborio risotto rice
200 ml / 7 fl. oz / ¾ cup white wine
500 ml / 17 fl. oz / 2 cups vegetable stock, warm
50 g / 1 ¾ oz / ½ cup Parmesan cheese, grated
200 g / 7 oz / 1 ⅓ cup chestnut mushrooms, chopped

METHOD

1. Heat half the oil in a lidded pan over a medium heat. Add the onion. Fry for 3 minutes. Add the garlic. Fry for 1 more minute.
2. Add half the butter and the rice and stir to coat. Turn the heat up and add the wine. Allow to bubble for 5 minutes. Turn the heat back down to a medium heat.
3. Add the stock to the rice, placing the lid on the pan after each addition. Check that the liquid has been absorbed each time before adding more stock to the pan. It will be ready when the rice is cooked but still has a slight bite. Stir through the remaining butter and grated cheese once the risotto is cooked.
4. Heat the remaining oil in a pan over a mid-high heat. Add the chopped mushrooms and cook for 8 minutes. Stir the cooked mushrooms through the risotto rice and serve.

Courgetti salad

SERVES: 2 | PREP TIME: 20 MINUTES | COOKING TIME: 10 MINUTES

INGREDIENTS

2 tbsp olive oil

2 courgettes (zucchinis)

2 cups chestnut mushrooms, quartered

½ cup pomegranate seeds

1 tomato, quartered

2 sprigs of fresh basil, to serve

METHOD

1. Heat a tablespoon of olive oil in a frying pan over a low-medium heat.
2. Prepare the courgettes by using either a spiralizer or julienne finely. Discard the centre with the seeds.
3. Lightly sauté the mushrooms until just browned. Toss together with the prepared courgette in a separate bowl before serving on plates.
4. Sprinkle the pomegranate seeds over the plate with a drizzle of fresh oil. Top with the tomatoes and basil.

Italian farro salad

SERVES: 2 | PREP TIME: 15 MINUTES | COOKING TIME: 20 MINUTES

INGREDIENTS

2 tbsp olive oil, plus more to drizzle
1 shallot, diced
1 clove of garlic, minced
100 g / 3 ½ oz / ¾ cup Italian farro
300 ml / 10 ½ fl. oz / 1 ¼ vegetable stock
100 g / 3 ½ oz / ½ cup asparagus tips
100 g / 3 ½ oz / ½ cup cherry tomatoes, halved
75 g / 2 ½ oz provolone cheese, cubed
50 g / 1 ¾ oz rocket (arugula) leaves

METHOD

1. Heat the oil in a pan with a lid over a medium heat. Add the shallot. Cook for 4 minutes. Add the garlic. Fry for 1 more minute.
2. Add the farro to the pan and stir through to coat in the oil before pouring in the stock. Bring to the boil then cover and reduce to a simmer. Cook for 15 minutes. Drain off any excess liquid, season and set aside.
3. To cook the asparagus, bring a salted pan of water to the boil. Add the asparagus and cook for 5 minutes until softened, drain and plunge into cold water to stop them cooking further.
4. To prepare the salad, combine the cooked farro with the asparagus, cherry tomatoes, cheese and rocket. Drizzle with olive oil.
5. Toss to combine and add to serving plates.

Artichoke antipasti

SERVES: 4 | PREP TIME: 10 MINUTES | COOKING TIME: 45 MINUTES

INGREDIENTS

4 globe artichokes

lemon juice

FOR THE VINAIGRETTE:

1 tsp salt

1 clove of garlic, crushed

1 tsp Dijon mustard

1 tbsp balsamic vinegar

black pepper

6 tbsp extra virgin olive oil

METHOD

1. Remove around 4-5 of the toughest outer leaves. Snap away the stem. Spread the leaves apart until you come to the central thinner, lighter leaves. Pull this cone out in one piece. Underneath will be the hairy choke. Scrape it out with a teaspoon.
2. Rinse the artichokes with water. Place in a bowl of water with lemon juice to prevent discolouring.
3. To cook the artichokes, bring water to the boil with some lemon juice and cook, uncovered, for about 30 minutes or until the bases are tender when tested with a skewer.
4. Whisk together the first 5 vinaigrette ingredients to a smooth paste and then stir in the olive oil.
5. To eat the artichokes, serve at room temperature, tear off a leaf at a time, dip it into vinaigrette and eat the tender base. Discard the rest of the leaf.

Caprese stuffed tomatoes

SERVES: 6 | PREP TIME: 10 MINUTES | COOKING TIME: 40 MINUTES

INGREDIENTS

6 large beef tomatoes

3 yellow tomatoes

3 green tomatoes

2 balls of buffalo mozzarella

100 g / 4 oz / ⅔ cup black olives, stoned

2 tbsp olive oil

salt and pepper

3 sprigs of basil

METHOD

1. Slice the tops off the beef tomatoes and hollow out with a teaspoon.
2. Sprinkle the insides with a little salt and leave to drain upside down for 30 minutes, then pat dry.
3. Cut the yellow and green tomatoes into small chunks.
4. Dice the mozzarella.
5. Mix them together with the olives, olive oil, seasoning and basil.
6. Spoon the mixture into the beef tomatoes and serve at room temperature.

Avocado with tomato and feta

SERVES: 4 | PREP TIME: 20 MINUTES

INGREDIENTS

2-3 ripe vine grown tomatoes
extra virgin olive oil
100 g / 3 ½ oz / ⅔ cup feta
2 tbsp black olives, stoned
basil leaves
salt and pepper
2 ripe avocados
juice of ½ lemon, optional

METHOD

1. Finely chop the tomatoes and place in a bowl. Season and drizzle with olive oil then leave to marinate for 10 minutes.
2. Dice the feta into small chunks, then add to the tomatoes, along with the olives. Tear up the basil leaves and add these too. Season to taste.
3. Cut the avocados in half when ready to serve and remove the stones.
4. Squeeze over a little lemon to prevent discolouring.
5. Fill the cavity in each avocado with the tomato and feta salad and serve.

Italian-style vegetables

SERVES: 8 | PREP TIME: 10 MINUTES | COOKING TIME: 40 MINUTES

INGREDIENTS

1 aubergine (eggplant)

2 courgettes (zucchinis)

2 red peppers, deseeded

2 onions, peeled

2 cloves garlic, whole

2 tbsp rosemary leaves, finely chopped

4 tbsp olive oil

METHOD

1. Preheat the oven to 200°C (180°C fan) / 400F / gas 6.
2. Slice the aubergine and courgettes into thick, even rounds of about 1 cm (½ in) width.
3. Cut the peppers into large pieces.
4. Slice the onions into thick rings.
5. Tip the vegetables into a roasting tin and toss with the garlic, rosemary and seasoning and drizzle with oil.
6. Roast for about 30-40 minutes until all is tender and golden.

Courgette mousse

SERVES: 4 | PREP TIME: 10 MINUTES | COOKING TIME: 25 MINUTES

INGREDIENTS

2 courgettes (zucchinis), very finely diced

1 egg, separated

1 heaped tbsp crème fraîche or double (heavy) cream

100 g / 3 ½ oz / ½ cup Gruyère or Parmesan, grated

salt and pepper

1 tbsp pesto

butter, for greasing the ramekins

2 tbsp pine nuts, lightly toasted

METHOD

1. Preheat the oven to 200°C (180°C fan) / 400F / gas 7.
2. Blanch the courgettes in boiling water for 3 minutes until tender.
3. Drain in a colander and then press lightly with a wooden spoon to extract excess water.
4. Whizz the courgettes in a blender with the egg yolk and crème fraîche until smooth.
5. Whisk the egg white to a stiff peak and then fold gradually into the courgette mixture. Stir through the pesto.
6. Spoon into greased ramekins then bake in the oven for about 20 minutes until set. Serve warm sprinkled with pine nuts.

Courgette and feta bread

SERVES: 6 | PREP TIME: 30 MINUTES | COOKING TIME: 35 MINUTES

INGREDIENTS

8 eggs

1 tbsp crème fraiche

2 courgettes (zucchinis), finely diced

handful of sun-dried tomatoes, finely chopped

100 g / 4 oz / ⅔ cup feta cheese, cubed

6 sprigs thyme

2 tbsp olive oil

METHOD

1. Preheat the oven to 180°C (160°C fan) / 350F / gas 4.
2. Beat the eggs with the crème fraiche in a large bowl.
3. Add the courgettes, tomatoes, feta, thyme leaves and season then mix together carefully.
4. Oil a large frying pan, then pour the mixture in and bake for about 35 minutes until puffed and golden. The egg should be cooked through.
5. Cut into squares and serve warm or cold.

Creamed pepper soup

SERVES: 4 | PREP TIME: 5 MINUTES | COOKING TIME: 45 MINUTES

INGREDIENTS

1 ciabatta loaf

olive oil

25 g / 1 oz butter

1 onion, finely chopped

1 clove of garlic, finely chopped

4 yellow peppers, finely chopped

750 ml / 1 ¼ pints / 3 cups chicken stock

120 ml / 4 fl oz / ½ cup double (heavy) cream

salt and pepper

METHOD

1. Preheat the oven to 180°C (160°C fan) / 350F / gas 5. Tear the ciabatta into large croutons and toss with olive oil. Place on a baking sheet.
2. Bake in the oven for 10-12 minutes, until golden and crunchy and then set aside on kitchen paper.
3. Heat the butter in a pan, then sweat the onion and garlic without colouring. Add the peppers. Cook for a further 10 minutes until they soften. Pour over the stock. Simmer for 25 minutes, until the peppers are tender.
4. Allow to cool slightly and then whizz in a liquidizer until smooth.
5. Transfer back to the pan and stir in the cream, heating gently. Season, then serve.

Farfalle primavera

SERVES: 4 | PREP TIME: 5 MINUTES | COOKING TIME: 15 MINUTES

INGREDIENTS

70 g / 2 ½ oz / ⅓ cup farfalle pasta per person
olive oil
½ bunch asparagus, trimmed
100 g / 3 ½ oz / ½ cup peas, fresh or frozen
100 g / 3 ½ oz / ½ cup broad beans, double-podded
50 g / 1 ¾ oz butter
2 tsp Parmesan, grated
salt and pepper

METHOD

1. Cook the pasta in boiling salted water according to packet instructions. Drain, reserving a little of the cooking water, then toss with little olive oil to prevent sticking.
2. Meanwhile steam the asparagus until nearly tender. Check after 4 minutes, then keep checking until it is ready.
3. Cook the peas and beans for 2-3 minutes.
4. Heat the butter in a pan and add the vegetables. Cook for 1 minute then add the pasta and reserved water.
5. Toss together and then sprinkle over the Parmesan. Adjust the seasoning and serve.

Grilled red peppers

SERVES: 2 | PREP TIME: 5 MINUTES | COOKING TIME: 10 MINUTES

INGREDIENTS

4 red peppers
extra virgin olive oil
salt and pepper

METHOD

1. Preheat a grill to very hot or open up a gas flame to full.
2. Roast the peppers under the grill or over the flame until completely blackened and blistered all over.
3. Place the peppers in a plastic bag and seal and set aside.
4. Once cool, peel the skin away from the flesh but try to keep the flesh intact.
5. Season and drizzle with olive oil.
6. Serve with ciabatta to mop up the juices.

Salad with soft-boiled egg dressing

SERVES: 6 | PREP TIME: 30 MINUTES | COOKING TIME: 25 MINUTES

INGREDIENTS

2 red peppers

2 yellow peppers

175 g / 6 oz / ¾ cup rocket (arugula) leaves

120 g / 4 ½ oz / ⅔ cup sun-dried tomatoes

Parmesan, to shave

6 eggs

2 tbsp olive oil

2 tbsp balsamic vinegar

3 thick slices granary bread, cut in half

METHOD

1. Cut the peppers in half and discard the seeds and white pith.
2. Lay the peppers on a baking sheet and grill until completely blackened. Remove from the heat, place in a plastic bag and leave to cool.
3. Peel the skin away from the peppers and roughly chop the flesh.
4. Place in a bowl with the rocket, tomatoes and some shaved Parmesan and set aside.
5. Cook the eggs in boiling water for 6 minutes. Remove, leave to cool a little then peel away the shell.
6. Dress the salad with the olive oil and balsamic vinegar. Season well.
7. Serve the salad with the egg just broken in half on top and the bread alongside.

Vegetable tart

SERVES: 6 | PREP TIME: 40 MINUTES | COOKING TIME: 40-45 MINUTES

INGREDIENTS

FOR THE TART:
2 x 375 g packs ready-rolled shortcrust pastry
1 egg, beaten

FOR THE FILLING:
olive oil
1 onion, peeled and finely chopped
2 cloves of garlic, finely sliced
1 aubergine (eggplant), cut into thin slices
2 courgettes (zucchinis), cut into thin slices
1 jar roasted red peppers
2 eggs, beaten
275 ml / 10 fl oz / 1 cup double (heavy) cream
salt and pepper

METHOD

1. Preheat the oven to 180°C (160°C fan) / 350F / gas 4. Roll out 1 pastry sheet. Use to line a pie dish.
2. Heat the oil in a pan and cook the onion and garlic until golden. Move from the pan to a bowl using a slotted spoon. Add the aubergine and a drop of oil and cook until tender. Place them on kitchen paper. Repeat with the courgette slices.
3. Layer the vegetables with the peppers in the base of the pie dish,alternating the layers.
4. Whisk together the eggs and cream, season and pour over the vegetables.
5. Roll out the remaining pastry sheet and cut into 1 cm wide strips. Use them to form a lattice on top of the pie. Bake in the oven for around 35-40 minutes until the pastry is golden. Serve warm.

Stuffed mushrooms

SERVES: 4 | PREP TIME: 5 MINUTES | COOKING TIME: 20 MINUTES

INGREDIENTS

4 large flat mushrooms
salt and pepper
olive oil
100 g / 3 ½ oz / ½ cup Gorgonzola
2 tbsp mascarpone
handful flat-leaf parsley
rocket (arugula) salad, to serve

METHOD

1. Season and drizzle the mushrooms with a little oil, then grill until tender.
2. Mix together the cheeses and parsley.
3. Spoon on top of the mushrooms and grill until the cheese is bubbling.
4. Serve with a rocket salad.

Olive and tomato focaccia

SERVES: 2 | PREP TIME: 2 HOURS 40 MINUTES | COOKING TIME: 20 MINUTES

INGREDIENTS

760 g / 1 lb 10 oz/ 5 cups '00' flour (Italian super-white flour)
½ tsp salt
150 ml / 5 fl. oz / ⅔ cup olive oil
2 tsp fast-action dried yeast
450 ml / 16 fl. oz / 1 ⅘ cups lukewarm water
150 g / 5 oz / 1 cup cherry tomatoes
150 g / 5 oz / ⅔ cup mixed green and black olives, pitted
handful of rosemary leaves

METHOD

1. Sift the flour and salt into a bowl. Make a well. Pour one third of the oil into the flour, add the yeast and rub together. Pour in ¾ of the water and mix to bring the dough together.
2. Tip the dough onto a floured surface and knead for 10 minutes. Place in an oiled bowl. Cover with film. Leave to rise for 1 hour 30 minutes.
3. Then, knock back the dough and divide it into two balls then roll them into 2 circles. Place in oiled pizza pans. Cover. Leave for 30 minutes.
4. Preheat the oven to 200°C (180°C fan) / 400F / gas 6. Uncover the dough. Push your fingertips in at regular intervals to make deep dimples. Drizzle with oil so that the dimples fill up.
5. Top with tomatoes, olives and rosemary. Spray with a little water. Bake for 20 minutes. Drizzle with oil. Transfer to a wire rack to cool then serve.

Spring vegetable penne

SERVES: 4 | PREP TIME: 10 MINUTES | COOKING TIME: 15 MINUTES

INGREDIENTS

500 g / 1lb / 2 cups penne pasta

2 tbsp butter, or olive oil

100 g / 3 ½ oz / ½ cup broccoli

8 asparagus stalks, woody ends snapped off and cut into short lengths

2 tsp Parmesan, grated

METHOD

1. Cook the pasta in boiling salted water according to packet instructions.
2. Meanwhile heat the butter or oil in a pan and add the vegetables with a splash of pasta cooking water.
3. Cook gently until the broccoli and asparagus is just tender.
4. Drain the pasta and toss with the vegetables and keep warm.
5. Serve with grated Parmesan.

Antipasti

SERVES: 4 | PREP TIME: 30-60 MINUTES

INGREDIENTS

4 red peppers
1 aubergine (eggplant)
2-3 tbsp extra virgin olive oil
1 tbsp balsamic vinegar
salt and pepper
1 tbsp pine nuts, lightly toasted
Parmesan shavings

METHOD

1. Preheat a grill to very hot or open up a gas flame to full. Roast the peppers under the grill or over the flame until blistered all over.
2. Place the peppers in a plastic bag. Seal and set aside. Repeat the process with the aubergine.
3. Slice the aubergine in half and scoop out the middle into a bowl. Discard the skin.
4. Dress the aubergine with olive oil and balsamic vinegar and season. Peel the skin off the peppers. It should come away easily, but try to keep the flesh whole.
5. Lay the roasted peppers flat on a serving platter along with any juices from the bag. Spoon the aubergine around. Scatter over pine nuts and Parmesan before serving at room temperature.

Polenta and courgette millefoglie

SERVES: 4 | PREP TIME: 35-40 MINUTES | COOKING TIME: 55 MINUTES

INGREDIENTS

225 g / 9 oz / 1 cup polenta

1.7 litres / 3 pints / 6 cups water

2 tbsp olive oil

2 courgettes (zucchinis), finely diced

4 tbsp pine nuts, lightly toasted

6 mint leaves, finely sliced

zest of ½ lemon

METHOD

1. Whisk the polenta slowly in a pan of boiling water. Once it begins to boil, cover with a lid askew and turn the heat down to minimum.
2. When it begins to thicken, stir every 5 minutes. Cook for 45 minutes until it begins to have the consistency of mashed potato. Season generously.
3. Oil a tray and tip the polenta out onto it. Spread the polenta to about 2.5cm thick. Leave the polenta to cool for about 30 minutes and then cut into rectangles about 6cm x 4cm.
4. Heat the oil in a pan. Fry the courgettes until tender. Stir in the pine nuts, mint and lemon zest.
5. Spoon onto a polenta rectangle, top with another rectangle, and repeat. Set aside. Repeat until the entire filling is used up.

Pumpkin and tomato pizzas

SERVES: 3-4 | PREP TIME: 1 HOUR 20 MINUTES | COOKING TIME: 30 MINUTES

INGREDIENTS

FOR THE DOUGH:

400 g / 14 oz / 2 ⅔ cups strong white bread flour

100 g / 3 ½ oz / ⅔ cup fine ground semolina flour

½ tbsp salt

½ tbsp dried yeast

½ tbsp caster (superfine) sugar

350ml / 12 fl. oz / 1 ⅖ cups lukewarm water

FOR THE TOPPING:

1 medium pumpkin, halved and deseeded (or butternut squash)

1 tbsp olive oil

20 cherry tomatoes, halved

2 balls mozzarella

handful of basil leaves

METHOD

1. To make the pizza, pour the flours and salt into a bowl and make a well in the centre, add the yeast and sugar to the water, mix with a fork and leave for a few minutes.
2. Bring in all the flour, mixing well. When it comes together, pat it into a ball with your hands.
3. Knead the dough for around 10 minutes until the dough is smooth and elastic, cover with film and leave to rest for 30 minutes.
4. Preheat the oven to 240°C (220°C fan) / 475F / gas 9.
5. Cut the pumpkin into small chunks and roast for about 20 minutes in the oven with the olive oil until tender and caramelized.
6. Roll the pizzas out about 30 minutes before you want to cook them. Then flour the surface, tear off a piece of dough and roll into a rough circle of about 1 cm (½ in) thick.
7. Top each pizza with some of the pumpkin, halved tomatoes and small pieces of mozzarella.
8. Place either directly on the bars of the oven or on a preheated baking sheet for 8-10 minutes until golden and crisp. Sprinkle with basil leaves before serving.

Pumpkin gnocchi

SERVES: 6 | PREP TIME: 10 MINUTES | COOKING TIME: 50 MINUTES

INGREDIENTS

400 g / 13 ½ oz / 1 ½ cups pumpkin, peeled

250 g / 9 oz / 1 cup potatoes, peeled

2 eggs

500 g / 1 lb / 2 cups plain (all-purpose) flour

salt and pepper

METHOD

1. Cut the pumpkin and potato into cubes and steam for 30-45 minutes, until tender.
2. Push through a potato ricer to make a smooth purée, or mash thoroughly until there are no lumps.
3. Add the eggs, mix well, then add the flour and stir until combined. The mixture should be fairly stiff – you should be able to shape it.
4. Form into small balls and press down on one side with a fork to give the gnocchi shape.
5. Bring a large pan of salted water to the boil and tip in the gnocchi. When they float to the surface, they are cooked. Remove with a slotted spoon and leave to drain on kitchen paper.
6. Re-heat immediately in a pan, with butter and Parmesan or your favourite pasta sauce.

Zingy summer salad

SERVES: 1 | PREP TIME: 15 MINUTES | COOKING TIME: 25 MINUTES

INGREDIENTS

50 g / 1.5 oz. / ¼ cup Camargue red rice

50 g / 1 ½ oz curly leaf kale

1 lemon, juice

1 tsp extra virgin olive oil

1 tsp sea salt

½ blood orange

25 g / 1 oz pomegranate seeds

25 g / 1 oz hazelnuts (cob nuts), roughly chopped

1 tsp sunflower seeds

1 tbsp cottage cheese

METHOD

1. Soak the rice and then add to a saucepan and top up with double the volume of water. Bring to the boil and then cover and simmer for 20 minutes until cooked. Drain well and rinse.
2. Remove the tough stem from the kale and chop into bite-sized pieces. Place in a bowl with the lemon, oil and salt and squeeze the leaves to soften them. Set aside whilst the rice cooks.
3. Peel the orange and remove the white pith. Using a knife, remove the fleshy segment and add to the kale.
4. Add the rice to a bowl and top with the other ingredients for a refreshing and tasty salad.

Polenta lentil croquettes

SERVES: 4 | PREP TIME: 10-15 MINUTES | COOKING TIME: 40-45 MINUTES

INGREDIENTS

200 g / 7 oz / 1 cup green lentils
1 tbsp miso paste, dissolved in
750 ml / 1 pint 6 fl. oz / 3 cups hot water
110 g / 4 oz / ⅔ cup cornflour
110 g / 4 oz / 1 cup smoked tempeh
55 g / 2 oz / ½ cup bulgar wheat
1.2 l / 2 pints / 5 ½ cups vegetable oil
plain (all-purpose) flour, to dust
2 medium eggs, beaten
200 g / 7 oz / 1 cup polenta
2 chicory bulbs, leaves removed
1 tbsp sunflower seeds
small handful of micro salad
1 tsp chilli (chili) flakes

METHOD

1. Combine the lentils, miso and hot water mixture in a pan. Bring to the boil over a moderate heat and cook for 10 minutes before reducing to a simmer for 15-20 minutes.
2. Remove from the heat and mash until smooth. Spoon into a bowl and add the cornflower and tempeh, then cover and chill.
3. Place the bulgar in a pan and cover with boiling water. Cook over a very low heat, until the grains are plump and tender. Drain if necessary.
4. Heat the oil in a saucepan to 180°C / 350F gas 4.
5. Spoon the lentil mixture and shape into croquettes. Dust in the flour then dip in the beaten egg. Coat in the polenta before arranging on lined trays.
6. Deep-fry in the hot oil until golden. Drain on kitchen paper and spoon the bulgar into the chicory leaves, arranging next to the croquettes.
7. Garnish the bulgar with sunflower seeds, salad and a pinch of chilli flakes before serving.

Penne with tomato and olives

SERVES: 4 | PREP TIME: 2 MINUTES | COOKING TIME: 12 MINUTES

INGREDIENTS

400 g / 14 oz / 4 cups penne
100 ml / 3 ½ fl. oz / ½ cup olive oil
2 cloves of garlic, crushed
6 anchovy fillets in oil
400 g / 14 oz / 2 cups canned plum tomatoes
½ tsp dried oregano
150 g / 5 ½ oz / 1 cup mixed pitted olives, drained
75 g / 2 ½ oz Pecorino Romano, in one piece
4 sprigs basil, to garnish

METHOD

1. Boil the pasta according to the packet instructions.
2. Meanwhile, heat the oil in a sauté pan with the garlic and anchovies, stirring until the anchovies dissolve.
3. Add the tomatoes and let it come to a simmer. Stir in the oregano and olives.
4. Drain the pasta and stir it into the sauce. Divide between four bowls, then use a vegetable peeler to shave over the Pecorino.
5. Garnish with basil and serve immediately.

Stuffed red peppers

SERVES: 4 | PREP TIME: 10 MINUTES | COOKING TIME: 50 MINUTES

INGREDIENTS

4 red peppers
4 tsp olive oil
100 g / 4 oz / ½ cup risotto rice
1 red bell pepper, chopped
2 cups broccoli florets
1 small courgette (zucchini), chopped
1 cup mixed olives, sliced
500 ml / 18 fl. oz / 2 cup vegetable stock
2 sprigs thyme, roughly chopped

METHOD

1. Preheat the oven to 180°C (160°C fan) / 350F / gas 4.
2. Cook the peppers for 4 minutes in boiling water, or until just softened.
3. Heat the olive oil. Fry the rice over a low heat, stirring frequently for 2 minutes before adding the remaining vegetables. Continue for 2 more minutes.
4. Pour in the stock and cook for 15 minutes, stirring until the rice is tender.
5. Drain off any excess liquid, then stir in the thyme. Season. Spoon the stuffing into the peppers and then place in a roasting tin.
6. Bake in the oven for about 20 minutes or until the peppers are tender and the stuffing is hot.

Mushroom tomato salad

SERVES: 4 | PREP TIME: 5 MINUTES | COOKING TIME: 30 MINUTES

INGREDIENTS

400 g / 13 ½ oz / 1 ½ cups button mushrooms, brushed clean

300 g / 10 oz / 1 ¼ cups cherry tomatoes, preferably on the vine

3 tbsp olive oil

4 cloves garlic, lightly crushed

FOR THE DRESSING:

4 tbsp extra virgin olive oil

1 tbsp balsamic vinegar

1 sprig lemon thyme

METHOD

1. Preheat the oven to 200°C (180°C fan) / 400F / gas 7.
2. Place the mushrooms and tomatoes in a roasting tin and toss with the oil. Arrange the garlic cloves around the vegetables.
3. Roast in the oven for about 30 minutes.
4. Tip the contents of the pan into a serving bowl, reserving the cooking juices.
5. Pour the cooking juices into a bowl. Pick out the garlic cloves and squeeze into the bowl.
6. Whisk in a little more extra virgin olive oil and the balsamic.
7. Add the thyme then gently toss the warm vegetables in the dressing.

Mushroom ravioli

SERVES: 6 | PREP TIME: 45 MINUTES | COOKING TIME: 3-4 MINUTES

CHILLING TIME: 30 MINUTES

INGREDIENTS

FOR THE PASTA:
500 g / 1 lb 2 oz / 3 ⅓ cups '00' flour
6 eggs

FOR THE FILLING:
3 tbsp butter
200 g / 7 oz / 1 cup wild mushrooms, brushed clean
150 g / 5 oz / 2 cups flat mushrooms, finely chopped
2 tbsp Parmesan, grated
1 tbsp flat-leaved parsley, finely chopped

TO GARNISH:
butter
Parmesan, grated

METHOD

1. Place the flour in a bowl and make a well in the centre. Crack the eggs into the well. Beat the eggs, then draw in the flour until the dough comes together. Knead the dough for 5 minutes. Cover with film and chill for 30 minutes in the refrigerator.
2. Heat the butter and sweat the mushrooms. Stir in the Parmesan and parsley and season.
3. Using a pasta machine, roll the dough into sheets 2 mm thick and 10 cm wide. Lay on a floured surface. Place 1 teaspoon of filling in the middle of the sheet at one end. Repeat all the way along at 5 cm intervals and then brush a little water in a circle, around each filling.
4. Place another sheet of pasta on top, then push the sheets together and around each mound of filling. Cut the ravioli into shapes.
5. Bring a pan of water to the boil. Cook for 3 minutes. Remove with a slotted spoon then toss with more butter and Parmesan to serve.

Tomatoes with ratatouille

SERVES: 2 | PREP TIME: 35 MINUTES | COOKING TIME: 1 HOUR

INGREDIENTS

8 tbsp olive oil
1 small aubergine (eggplant), finely chopped
1 red pepper, seeded and finely chopped
2 courgettes (zucchinis), finely chopped
2 tomatoes, chopped
100 g / 3 ½ oz / ½ cup black olives, stoned
2 sprigs of basil
8 tomatoes
salt and pepper

METHOD

1. Heat half the oil in a large pan then add the aubergine and pepper and cook for 10 minutes.
2. Add the courgettes, stir, reduce the heat and cook for a further 10 minutes. Add the chopped tomatoes, cover and cook for 15 minutes.
3. Cut the olives into rounds and then add to the pan with the basil.
4. Preheat the oven to 210°C / 420F / gas 7.
5. Take the tops off the tomatoes and hollow out with a teaspoon. Place in a roasting tin and fill each one with ratatoutille. Place the tops back on, drizzle with the rest of the oil and cook in the oven for about 25 minutes.
6. Serve hot or warm.

Cheese gnocchi

SERVES: 4 | PREP TIME: 1 HOUR | COOKING TIME: 10 MINUTES

INGREDIENTS

700 g / 1 ½ lb floury potatoes, such as Maris Piper, peeled

250 g / 8 oz / 2 cups plain (all-purpose) flour

1 egg, beaten

nutmeg, grated to taste

4 tbsp butter

3 tbsp Parmesan, grated

100 g / 3 ½ oz / ½ cup Gruyère cheese, grated

METHOD

1. Boil the potatoes in boiling water for at least 25 minutes until tender all the way through.
2. Drain and mash until smooth. Leave to cool.
3. Tip the potatoes into a bowl. Work in the flour, egg and nutmeg until you have a smooth dough.
4. Cut the dough in half. Roll it out to make 2 fat sausages. Cut into pieces about 3cm long. Press down with a fork to make the traditional indentations. Place on a floured baking sheet to cook when ready.
5. Bring a pan of water to the boil then add the gnocchi. When they float, they are ready, so remove and drain on kitchen paper.
6. Heat the butter in a pan. Toss the gnocchi in the butter. Tip into a baking dish and scatter with Parmesan and Gruyère. Grill until golden.

Roasted aubergine with tomatoes

SERVES: 4 | PREP TIME: 25 MINUTES | COOKING TIME: 30 MINUTES

INGREDIENTS

2 large aubergines (eggplants) or 4 small ones

salt

2 tbsp olive oil

4 tomatoes, chopped

1 tbsp balsamic vinegar

METHOD

1. Preheat the oven to 200°C (180°C fan) / 400F / gas 6.
2. Slice the aubergines in half lengthways. Cut the flesh into a cross hatch with a small sharp knife, then salt lightly and leave upside down for 20 minutes. This will help them absorb less oil.
3. Turn the aubergines right way up and pat dry. Drizzle generously with oil, then top with tomatoes and season with black pepper.
4. Roast in the oven for about 30 minutes, or until the flesh is completely tender and the tomatoes have sunk into the aubergines.
5. Drizzle with a little balsamic before serving.

Italian tomato soup

SERVES: 4-6 | PREP TIME: 15 MINUTES | COOKING TIME: 45 MINUTES

INGREDIENTS

75 ml / 2 ½ fl. oz / ⅓ cup extra virgin olive oil
1 large onion, diced
4 cloves of garlic, crushed
2 x 400 g / 14 oz / 2 cups canned Italian tomatoes
500 ml / 17 fl. oz / 2 cups vegetable stock
2 tsp dried oregano
handful of fresh basil leaves, chopped
sea salt and crushed mixed pepper
dill, to serve

METHOD

1. In a lidded saucepan, heat enough of the oil to coat the bottom of the pan over a medium heat. Add the onions then cook for 5 minutes. Add the garlic. Cook for 1 more minute.
2. Add the tomatoes, stock and oregano to the pan. Stir, turn up the heat to bring it to the boil then turn down to a simmer. Put the lid on the pan. Simmer for 30 minutes.
3. Add the remaining oil, basil and season with salt and pepper to taste. Using a hand or upright blender, blend the soup to a smooth consistency. Return to the heat. Cook on a low setting for a further 5 minutes.
4. To serve ladle into a soup bowl and add a frond of dill. Drizzle with oil or cream if desired.

Griddled courgette

SERVES: 4 | PREP TIME: 15 MINUTES | COOKING TIME: 5 MINUTES

INGREDIENTS

2 courgettes (zucchinis)
1 tbsp olive oil
150 g / 5 ¼ oz / ¾ cup ricotta
50 g / 1 ¾ oz crème fraîche
1 lemon, juice and zest
2 tbsp chives, chopped
sea salt and freshly ground black pepper
handful of flat-leaved parsley, chopped

METHOD

1. Using a sharp knife or mandoline, slice the courgette lengthways into 2 mm thick slices.
2. Brush with olive oil and season lightly with salt and pepper.
3. Heat a cast iron griddle pan over a medium high heat until smoking. Add the courgette slices to the pan and cook for 1 minute on each side. Only turn once.
4. To make the dip combine the ricotta, crème fraîche and lemon in a bowl and mix well to combine. Stir in the chives and season.
5. Serve the dip alongside the griddled courgette. Sprinkle over the parsley.

Roasted aubergines

SERVES: 4 | PREP TIME: 5 MINUTES | COOKING TIME: 25-30 MINUTES

INGREDIENTS

2 aubergines (eggplants)

2 tbsp olive oil

2 tsp dried oregano

METHOD

1. Preheat the oven to 200°C (180°C fan) / 400F / gas 6.
2. Slice the aubergines in half lengthways and place in a roasting tin. Using a sharp knife, score a cross hatch pattern into the flesh. This will help them cook more quickly.
3. Drizzle generously with good olive oil and season. Sprinkle over the oregano.
4. Roast in the oven for 25-30 minutes or until blackened and collapsed.
5. The flesh can now be scooped out and used as a dip or blended with yogurt or cream cheese for a milder flavour.

Mediterranean Salad

SERVES: 2 | PREP TIME: 20 MINUTES

INGREDIENTS

1 red pepper
1 yellow pepper
100 g / 3 ½ oz / ½ cup mixed cherry tomatoes
½ red onion
½ cucumber
50 g / 1 ¾ oz / ⅓ cup black olives
100 g / 3 ½ oz / ½ cup mini mozzarella balls
handful of flat-leaved parsley
2 tbsp extra virgin olive oil
sea salt and freshly ground black pepper

METHOD

1. Halve and deseed the peppers, removing the stalk. Roughly chop into cubes and add to a mixing bowl.
2. Halve the tomatoes. Slice the red onion and cucumber, then add to the peppers.
3. Place the olives and mozzarella balls into the bowl before tearing the parsley and adding.
4. Pour over the olive oil and season with salt and black pepper.
5. Toss the ingredients together in the bowl before placing on serving plates.

Red pepper involtini

SERVES: 4 | PREP TIME: 10 MINUTES | COOKING TIME: 30 MINUTES

INGREDIENTS

4 red peppers
olive oil

FOR THE FILLING
100 g / 3 ½ oz / ½ cup pine nuts
100 g / 3 ½ oz / ½ cup cream cheese
1 tbsp Parmesan, grated
½ bunch flat-leaved parsley
zest of 1 lemon
salt and pepper

METHOD

1. Preheat the oven to 200°C (180°C fan) / 400 F/ gas 7.
2. Seed and core the pepper and then roast whole with a little oil until tender.
3. Open out the peppers and cut each one into 2 rectangles and set aside.
4. Toast three-quarters of the pine nuts in a dry frying pan until golden. Add to a food processor with the cream cheese, Parmesan, parsley, zest and seasoning. Whizz until smooth, then stir in the whole pine nuts.
5. Spoon the filling down one side of each pepper rectangle, then roll the pepper up to make a roulade.
6. Serve at room temperature.

Avocado cucumber salad

SERVES: 1 | PREP TIME: 15 MINUTES

INGREDIENTS

1 gem lettuce

½ cucumber

1 avocado

handful of basil leaves, chopped

1 tbsp linseeds

1 tbsp extra virgin olive oil

sea salt and freshly ground black pepper

METHOD

1. Halve and roughly chop the lettuce and place into a bowl.
2. Peel the cucumber and cut into half lengthways. Scrape out the seeds before roughly chopping and adding to the lettuce.
3. Chop the avocado in half and remove the stone. Scoop out the flesh and roughly chop before adding to the bowl.
4. Toss the lettuce, cucumber and avocado together adding the basil leaves and seasoning.
5. Place the combined salad ingredients to a plate before scattering over the seeds and drizzling with the olive oil. Season again and serve with some crusty bread.

Rustic tomato pizza

SERVES: 2 | PREP TIME: 1 HOUR | COOKING TIME: 15 MINUTES

INGREDIENTS

FOR THE DOUGH:

1 tsp active dried yeast
1 tbsp caster (superfine) sugar
200 g / 7 oz / 1 ⅓ cup bread flour
pinch of salt
1 large free-range egg, beaten
100 ml / 3 ½ fl. oz / ½ cup semi-skimmed milk
2 tbsp olive oil
½ teaspoon bicarbonate of (baking) soda
2 tsp white wine vinegar

FOR THE TOPPING:

100 g / 3 ½ oz / ½ cup passata
2 tsp dried oregano
250 g / 9 oz / 1 cup mozzarella
2 tomatoes, sliced
handful of basil leaves

METHOD

1. Mix the yeast and sugar with 50ml lukewarm water. Cover and set aside to allow the yeast to activate; it should start to foam.
2. In a mixing bowl, combine the flour with a little salt. Mix the egg, milk and oil in a jug. Create a well in the centre of the flour then pour in the milk and yeast mixtures. Bring together until a dough forms.
3. Combine the bicarbonate of soda and vinegar, then quickly add to the dough and knead. Place the dough into a lightly oiled bowl, cover and leave in a warm place for an hour or until doubled in size.
4. Preheat the oven to 240°C (220°C fan) / 475F / gas 9 and lightly grease two baking trays.
5. Divide the dough into two and roll out to roughly the same size as the baking tray. Transfer to the trays. Stretch to fill the space.
6. Ladle over the passata and sprinkle over the oregano. Tear the mozzarella and place on the pizza bases with the sliced tomatoes and a scattering of basil leaves.
7. Place into the hot oven for 12-15 minutes until the base is golden and the cheese is melted.

Spinach risotto

SERVES: 2 | PREP TIME: 10 MINUTES | COOKING TIME: 30 MINUTES

INGREDIENTS

1 onion, diced
2 cloves garlic, minced
2 tbsp butter
300 g / 10 ½ oz / 1 ½ cup Arborio risotto rice
150 ml / 5 fl. oz / ⅔ cup white wine
500 ml / 17 fl. oz / 2 cups vegetable stock, warm
50 g / 1 ¾ oz / ½ cup Parmesan cheese, grated
200 g / 7 oz / 1 cup spinach, washed
100 g / 3 ½ oz / ½ cup ricotta cheese
100 ml / 3 ½ fl. oz / ½ cup double (heavy) cream
sea salt and freshly ground black pepper

METHOD

1. Heat some oil in a lidded pan over a medium heat. Add onion with a pinch of salt. Fry for 3 minutes. Add the garlic. Fry for 1 more minute.
2. Add the butter and rice to the pan. Stir through to coat the rice with the butter and oil. Turn the heat up a little and add the wine. Allow to cook and bubble for 5 minutes. Turn the heat back down to a medium heat.
3. Add the stock to the rice, placing the lid on the pan after each addition. Check that the liquid has been absorbed each time before adding further stock to the pan. It will be ready when the rice is cooked but still has a slight chalky bite. Season to taste.
4. Place the Parmesan, spinach, ricotta and cream into a blender and blend for a minute until combined. Stir through the cooked risotto until fully coated and serve.

Three-cheese risotto

SERVES: 2 | PREP TIME: 10 MINUTES | COOKING TIME: 30 MINUTES

INGREDIENTS

2 tbsp olive oil
1 leek, finely sliced
1 celery stick, diced
1 clove of garlic, minced
300 g / 10 ½ oz / 1 ½ cup risotto rice
150 ml / 5 fl. oz / ⅔ cup white wine
500 ml / 17 fl. oz / 2 cups chicken stock
100 g / 3 ½ oz / ½ cup Gruyère cheese, chopped
75 g / 2 ½ oz taleggio cheese, chopped
50 g / 1 ¾ oz / ½ cup Parmesan cheese, grated
salt and ground black pepper
micro herbs, to garnish

METHOD

1. Heat the oil in a heavy bottomed pan over a medium heat. Add the leek and celery to the pan. Fry for 5 minutes until softened. Add the garlic. Cook for 1 more minute until fragrant.
2. Add the rice to the pan and turn up the heat. Stir continuously to coat the rice in the other ingredients. Add the wine to the pan and allow to bubble and reduce in volume by half.
3. Turn the heat back down and add the chicken stock a ladleful at a time. Wait for the liquid to be absorbed each time before adding more. Continue to do this until the rice is cooked but still has a little bite to it.
4. Add the cheese to the rice and stir through until it has melted into the risotto, season with salt and black pepper before serving. Garnish with micro herbs and serve with some vegetables such as asparagus if desired.

Vegetable bake

SERVES: 4 | PREP TIME: 20 MINUTES | COOKING TIME: 40 MINUTES

INGREDIENTS

2 tbsp olive oil
1 aubergine (eggplant), sliced
1 tbsp flour
1 courgette (zucchini), sliced
2 tbsp green pesto
200 g / 7 oz / 1 cup ricotta
200 ml / 7 fl. oz / ¾ cup yogurt
1 tomato, sliced
2 tbsp capers
25 g / 1 oz black olives
sprig of basil, to serve
sea salt and ground black pepper

METHOD

1. Preheat the oven to 200°C (180°C fan) / 400F / gas 6
2. Heat the oil in a non-stick pan over a high heat. Coat the aubergine slices in the flour. Fry them for 3 minutes on each side. Remove. Set aside.
3. Fry the courgette slices in the pan for 2-3 minutes on each side until starting to colour. Remove and place with the aubergine.
4. Mix the vegetables with the green pesto and then layer in an ovenproof dish. Mix the ricotta with the yogurt then pour over the vegetables.
5. Place the sliced tomatoes on top, and sprinkle over the capers and olives. Bake in the oven for 30 minutes, until the topping has set. Remove and garnish with a sprig of basil.

Tomato bruschetta

SERVES: 1 | PREP TIME: 10 MINUTES | COOKING TIME: 20 MINUTES

INGREDIENTS

1 tbsp olive oil
½ onion, diced
1 clove of garlic, minced
100 g / 3 ½ oz / ½ cup cherry tomatoes, chopped
1 tsp sugar
25 g / 1 oz mixed olives, chopped
½ ciabatta loaf, sliced lengthways
1 tbsp extra virgin olive oil
handful of fresh basil leaves

METHOD

1. Heat the olive oil in a saucepan over a medium heat. Add the onion and cook for 5 minutes until soft. Add the garlic and fry for a further minute until fragrant.
2. Add the chopped tomatoes to the pan with a splash of water, the sugar and olives. Continue to cook for 10-15 minutes or until the tomatoes have broken down.
3. Place the bread under a hot grill with the cut side facing up. Toast for 4-5 minutes until crisp, remove from the oven and drizzle with extra virgin olive oil.
4. Place the bread onto a serving plate and top with the tomato and olive sauce, before garnishing with basil and additional olives.

Cook's Corner
Irresistible Italian
Sides and snacks

Fried meatballs

SERVES: 2 | PREP TIME: 45 MINUTES | COOKING TIME: 20 MINUTES

INGREDIENTS

200 g / 7 oz / 1 cup lean pork mince
200 g / 7 oz / 1 cup veal mince
1 egg, beaten
50 g / 1 ¾ oz / ½ cup Parmesan cheese, finely grated
1 clove of garlic, minced
1 tsp dried oregano
1 red chilli (chili), finely chopped
1 tsp tomato purée
handful of fresh basil leaves, chopped
salt and freshly ground black pepper
oil, for frying

METHOD

1. Place all the ingredients into a large mixing bowl apart from the oil. Using your hands bring it all together until thoroughly combined.
2. Lightly flour your hands and take a small handful of the mixture and form into a meatball roughly the size of a golf ball. Place onto a plate and set aside until all the meatball mixture has been used.
3. Place into the fridge and leave to rest for 20-30 minutes before cooking.
4. Heat the oil in the deep fat fryer to around 180°C (160°C fan) / 350F / gas 4. Alternatively, fill a high-sided pan with enough oil for shallow fry the meatballs.
5. Cook the meatballs in batches for around 10 minutes each until crisp on the outside and golden in colour.

Berry bruschetta

SERVES: 2 | PREP TIME: 5 MINUTES | COOKING TIME: 5 MINUTES

INGREDIENTS

4 slices of crusty bread
250 g / 9 oz / 1 cup mascarpone
2 tbsp honey
100 g / 3 ½ oz / ⅔ cup blueberries, washed
100 g / 3 ½ oz / ⅔ cup blackberries, washed
mint leaves, to garnish

METHOD

1. Place the bread under a hot grill and toast on both sides for 2-3 minutes until golden. Remove and set aside.
2. Mix the mascarpone with the honey.
3. Spread the mascarpone on the toasted bread.
4. Top with the washed and dried berries and garnish with mint leaves.

Sweet focaccia

SERVES: 1 | PREP TIME: 30 MINUTES | COOKING TIME: 15 MINUTES

INGREDIENTS

345 g / 12 oz / 2 ⅓ cups plain (all-purpose) flour
1 tsp salt
1 tbsp caster (superfine) sugar
1 tbsp dried active yeast
2 tbsp olive oil
235 ml / 8 fl. oz / ¾ cup water
2 tbsp butter, melted

METHOD

1. In a mixing bowl, combine the flour, salt, sugar and yeast. Mix in the oil and the water.
2. Once the dough has formed, turn out onto a floured surface and knead until elastic. Oil a large bowl and place the dough inside, cover with a damp cloth and leave in a warm place for 20 minutes until risen.
3. Preheat the oven to 220°C (200°C fan) / 425F / gas 7.
4. Turn the dough out onto a greased baking tray and form into a rough rectangle shape. Dot the dough with holes using your finger before brushing over the melted butter.
5. Bake in the oven for 15 minutes or until golden, remove from the oven and serve warm. Dust with sugar or drizzle with honey, if desired.

Fig and goat's cheese bruschetta

SERVES: 2 | PREP TIME: 10 MINUTES | COOKING TIME: 5 MINUTES

INGREDIENTS

4 slices of ciabatta
1 tbsp extra virgin olive oil
50 g / 1 ¾ oz soft goat's cheese
4 ripe figs
1 tbsp honey

METHOD

1. Place the bread under a hot grill for 2-3 minutes on each side until golden brown.
2. Drizzle one side of the toasted bread with the oil.
3. Spread the goats cheese onto the oiled side of the toast slices.
4. Cut the figs into quarters and place on top of the cheese.
5. Drizzle over the honey and serve.

Arancini with pine kernels

MAKES: 18 | PREP TIME: 20 MINUTES | COOKING TIME: 10 MINUTES

INGREDIENTS

1 tbsp Parmesan, grated
4 tbsp pine nuts
275 g / 10 oz / 1 cup cooked Arborio rice, cold
1 tbsp plain (all-purpose) flour
1 egg, beaten
40 g / 1 ½ oz / ⅓ cup breadcrumbs
vegetable oil, for deep frying

METHOD

1. Stir the Parmesan through the risotto.
2. Toast the pine nuts in a dry pan until lightly golden. Stir through the rice.
3. Shape into equal balls.
4. Lay out the flour, egg and breadcrumbs on separate plates.
5. Dip the risotto balls into the flour, then the egg, then the breadcrumbs. Use one hand and keep the other clean for ease.
6. Heat the oil to 180°C / 400F or until a cube of bread sizzles when dropped in the oil. Fry the risotto balls until golden and crisp.
7. Serve hot or warm.

Italian bread

SERVES: 2 | PREP TIME: 10 MINUTES | COOKING TIME: 25 MINUTES

INGREDIENTS

450 ml / 1 pint / 2 cups water
210 g / 7 oz / ¾ cup chickpea (gram) flour
3 tbsp olive oil
½ tsp salt
1 tsp rosemary leaves, finely chopped
sea salt, to serve

METHOD

1. Mix the water with the flour, 1 tablespoon of oil and the salt in a large bowl.
2. Cover and leave to rest for 2 hours.
3. Preheat the oven to 200°C (180°C fan) / 400F / gas 6.
4. Heat a large ovenproof frying pan with the remaining oil.
5. Skim off any foam from the batter and stir in the rosemary.
6. Pour the batter into the pan and place in the oven for 25 minutes until brown and crisp.
7. Sprinkle with sea salt before serving.

Mozzarella panzerotti

SERVES: 4 | PREP TIME: 45-55 MINUTES | COOKING TIME: 5 MINUTES

INGREDIENTS

FOR THE DOUGH:

200 g / 6 ½ oz / ¾ cup strong white bread flour

50 g / 1 ½ oz / ⅓ cup fine ground semolina flour

¼ tbsp salt

½ x 7g sachet dried yeast

¼ tbsp caster (superfine) sugar

175 ml / ¼ pint / ¾ cup lukewarm water

FOR THE FILLING:

100 g / 3 ½ oz / ½ cup mozzarella cheese

200 ml / 6 ½ fl oz / ¾ cup passata

3 tbsp basil, chopped

vegetable oil, for deep frying

METHOD

1. For the pizza dough, pour the flours and salt into a bowl, making a well in the centre. Mix the yeast, sugar and water. Pour into the well. Bring the flour into the water. When it comes together, pat it into a ball. Knead for 10 minutes. Cover and leave for 30 minutes.
2. Chop the mozzarella cheese into small cubes then mix together all the filling ingredients.
3. Once the dough has risen, uncover it and pull it out, using your hands, until it is thin. Cut out 15 small circles with a cutter or an upturned cup. Place 1 teaspoon of the filling onto half of the pastry circle. Fold the other half over, pinching to seal. Repeat.
4. Heat the oil to 190°C / 375F. Deep-fry the panzerotti in batches for 5 minutes until puffed and golden. Drain on kitchen paper and season. Serve hot.

Mushroom crostini

MAKES: 40 | PREP TIME: 30-40 MINUTES | COOKING TIME: 8 MINUTES

INGREDIENTS

1 ficelle loaf
olive oil
250 g / 9 oz / 1 cup mushrooms
1 onion, peeled
2 tbsp butter
2 cloves of garlic, very finely chopped
nutmeg
salt and pepper
2 tbsp double (heavy) cream
juice of ½ lemon

METHOD

1. Preheat the oven to 180°C (160°C fan) / 350F / gas 5.
2. Slice the ficelle into rounds about 1 cm thick.
3. Dab each one with a little oil and bake in the oven for about 8 minutes until lightly golden and crisp.
4. Whizz the mushrooms and onion in a food processor until finely chopped.
5. Heat the butter in a pan and cook the mushrooms and onions with the garlic and nutmeg for about 25-30 minutes until all the water has evaporated.
6. Season and stir in enough cream just to bind. Add lemon juice to taste.
7. Top the crostini with the mushroom cream.

Ricotta fritters

SERVES: 6 | PREP TIME: 1 HOUR 25 MINUTES | COOKING TIME: 5 MINUTES

INGREDIENTS

3 large eggs
600 g / 1 lb 5 oz / 4 cups ricotta cheese
½ tsp paprika
125 g / 4 ½ oz / ¾ cup plain (all-purpose) flour
2 red peppers, seeded and finely diced
1 handful chives, finely chopped
vegetable oil, for frying
basil, to garnish

METHOD

1. Separate 2 eggs and place the whites in the refrigerator for later use.
2. Place the ricotta in a bowl, season with salt and pepper and add the paprika – whisk in 1 whole egg and the 2 yolks a little at a time.
3. Whisk in the flour and then combine until smooth. Cover with film and place in the refrigerator for 1 hour.
4. Whisk the reserved egg whites to stiff peaks with a pinch of salt.
5. Add the red pepper and chives to the ricotta mixture, then gently mix in the egg whites, being careful not to lose the air.
6. Heat the oil in a pan. Using a teaspoon dipped in hot water, dip teaspoons of the mixture into the oil and turn gently until golden all over. Do this in batches.
7. Remove to kitchen paper to drain and keep warm in a low oven until required.

Tomato and basil crostini

MAKES: 20 | PREP TIME: 10 MINUTES | COOKING TIME: 45 MINUTES

INGREDIENTS

10 cherry tomatoes
olive oil
sea salt and freshly ground black pepper
2 sprigs rosemary leaves, finely chopped
1 ficelle loaf
extra virgin olive oil
2 cloves of garlic, halved
1 bunch basil leaves

METHOD

1. Preheat the oven to 200°C (180°C fan) / 400F / gas 7. Place the cherry tomatoes in a roasting tin and drizzle with oil, salt and pepper. Sprinkle over the rosemary and roast in the oven for 25 minutes or until lightly charred.
2. Slice the ficelle into rounds about 1 cm (½ in) thick.
3. Dab each one with a little oil and bake in the oven until lightly golden and crisp, for about 8 minutes.
4. Rub the crostini with the garlic. Push the tomatoes to one side in the tin and lightly press each crostini into the roasting juices to soak into the bread a little.
5. Top each crostini with a sprig of basil and half a cherry tomato. Season as desired.

Breaded cheese balls

SERVES: 4 | PREP TIME: 25 MINUTES | COOKING TIME: 10-15 MINUTES

INGREDIENTS

10 slices white bread, crusts removed
125 g / 4 ½ oz / 1 cup mozzarella pearls
285 g / 10 oz jar artichoke hearts
6 tbsp plain (all-purpose) flour
3 eggs, beaten
10 tbsp vegetable oil, for frying

METHOD

1. Combine the bread with salt and pepper in a food processor to make breadcrumbs.
2. Drain the mozzarella pearls and artichoke hearts. Pat dry.
3. Tip the flour onto one plate and the eggs into a shallow bowl.
4. Coat the mozzarella pearls and artichokes in the breadcrumbs. Dunk the crumbed cheese and artichokes into the egg, then the flour, then the egg again.
5. Heat the oil in a pan until a cube of bread sizzles when dunked in.
6. Fry cheese and artichokes in the oil in batches, turning carefully, until golden and crisp on all sides.
7. Drain on kitchen paper and serve hot.

Italian gougères

MAKES: 12 | PREP TIME: 10 MINUTES | COOKING TIME: 45 MINUTES

INGREDIENTS

110 g / 4 oz / ⅔ cup plain (all-purpose) flour
½ tsp salt
½ tsp black pepper
½ tsp dried oregano
pinch cayenne pepper
250 ml / 9 fl oz / 1 cup milk
125 g / 4 ½ oz / 1 ⅙ sticks butter, cubed
6 eggs, 1 separated
2 tbsp Parmesan, grated
4 tbsp Gruyère, grated
4 tomatoes, sliced
handful of black olives, stoned and sliced
½ bunch basil leaves, chopped
2 tbsp milk

METHOD

1. Preheat the oven to 220°C (200°C fan) / 450F / gas 7.
2. Place the flour in a bowl with the salt, pepper, oregano and cayenne.
3. Add the milk and butter to a large pan and bring to the boil. When the butter melts, reduce the heat and tip in the seasoned flour.
4. Stir quickly with a wooden spoon, beating until the dough starts to come away from the sides of the pan and form a ball.
5. Remove the pan from the heat and tip into a large mixer bowl. Beat at a medium speed for 1 minute, then the eggs one at a time.
6. Beat in the cheeses.
7. Fill a piping bag with the mixture and use to pipe onto ungreased baking trays.
8. Lightly press a tomato slice, a few chopped olives and basil into the centre of each one.
9. Whisk the remaining egg yolk with the milk and lightly brush the gougères.
10. Bake for about 10 minutes, then reduce the heat to 150°C (130°C fan) / 300F / gas 2 and bake for a further 15 minutes, or until golden brown. Cool on wire racks before serving.

Bruschetta

SERVES: **6-8** | PREP TIME: **15 MINUTES** | COOKING TIME: **8 MINUTES**

INGREDIENTS

1 part-cooked ciabatta loaf

5 very ripe vine-grown tomatoes, room temperature

salt and pepper

2 cloves of garlic, halved

extra virgin olive oil

300 g / 10 oz / 1 ¼ cups mozzarella

handful of black olives, chopped

basil, to garnish

METHOD

1. Preheat the oven and bake the ciabatta loaf according to packet instructions. Once cooked, leave to cool.
2. When cool, cut the loaf into 1.5 cm thick slices.
3. Slice the tomatoes and sprinkle with salt.
4. Heat a griddle pan until very hot and lay the bread on the griddle. Rub the toasted side with the cut garlic and drizzle with olive oil.
5. Slice the mozzarella and lay with the tomatoes on the toasted bread and scatter with chopped olives.
6. Scatter over the basil before serving.

Confit tomatoes and baked ricotta

SERVES: 4 | PREP TIME: 25 MINUTES | COOKING TIME: 3 HOURS 35 MINUTES

INGREDIENTS

500 g/ 1 lb 2 oz / 3 ⅓ cups plum tomatoes, halved
6 cloves garlic, unpeeled
4 thyme and 4 rosemary sprigs
6 tbsp olive oil
500 g / 1 lb 2 oz / 3 ⅓ cups ricotta
2 eggs
1 tbsp Parmesan, grated
½ lemon, grated zest
1 tbsp oregano leaves, chopped

METHOD

1. Preheat the oven to 120°C (100°C fan) / 250F / gas ½. Place the tomatoes in a roasting tin. Scatter over the garlic and herbs, then drizzle with oil.
2. Slow-roast in the oven for 3 hours until shrivelled. They can be preserved in a sterilised jar covered in oil in the refrigerator.
3. Tip the ricotta into a bowl and stir with a wooden spoon to loosen slightly. Beat in the eggs one at a time, then add the Parmesan, zest and oregano.
4. Tip into a greased loaf tin and bake at 180°C (160°C) / 350F / gas 5 for 35 minutes or so until set. Leave to cool then tip out onto a serving platter.
5. Serve the ricotta with the tomatoes.

Garlic bread with cheese

SERVES: 4 | PREP TIME: 10 MINUTES | COOKING TIME: 45 MINUTES

INGREDIENTS

2 baguettes
120 g / 4 oz / 1 stick butter, softened
4 cloves garlic, crushed
1 tbsp parsley, finely chopped
225 g / 8 oz / 2 cups fontina cheese

METHOD

1. Slice the baguettes on a diagonal to get elongated slices.
2. Mix the butter thoroughly with the garlic and parsley.
3. Spread the butter thickly onto the bread.
4. Top with slices of cheese and flash under a hot grill until bubbling and golden.

Mozzarella arancini

SERVES: 4 | PREP TIME: 20 MINUTES | COOKING TIME: 10 MINUTES

INGREDIENTS

60 g / 2 oz / ¼ cup leftover risotto (Arborio) rice, cooked

1 tbsp Parmesan, grated

1 ball mozzarella, cut into small cubes

1 tbsp plain (all-purpose) flour

1 egg, beaten

4 tbsp breadcrumbs

vegetable oil, for deep frying

METHOD

1. Leave the leftover risotto to get completely cold – preferably refrigerated overnight.
2. Stir the Parmesan through the risotto.
3. Shape into equal balls, pushing a small cube of mozzarella into the centre of each one and shaping the rice around it.
4. Lay out the flour, egg and breadcrumbs on separate plates. Dip the risotto balls into the flour, then the egg, then the breadcrumbs. Use one hand and keep the other clean for ease.
5. Heat the oil and fry the risotto balls until golden and crisp all over. Serve hot or warm.

Mozzarella fritters

SERVES: 2 | PREP TIME: 10 MINUTES | COOKING TIME: 10-15 MINUTES

INGREDIENTS

6 slices white bread, crusts removed
salt and pepper
pinch dried chilli flakes
1 ball mozzarella
3 heaped tbsp plain (all-purpose) flour
2 eggs, beaten
vegetable oil, for frying

METHOD

1. Mix the bread with salt and pepper and the chilli flakes in a food processor to make breadcrumbs.
2. Slice the mozzarella into ½ cm (¼ in) slices.
3. Tip the flour onto one plate and the eggs into another. Coat the mozzarella slices in the breadcrumbs. Dunk the crumbed slices into the egg, then the flour, then the egg again.
4. Heat about 1 cm (½ in) depth of oil in a pan until a cube of bread sizzles when dunked in.
5. Fry the crumbed mozzarella in the oil, turning carefully, until golden and crisp on all sides.
6. Drain on kitchen paper and serve hot.

Spinach mozzarella cake

SERVES: 4 | PREP TIME: 25 MINUTES | COOKING TIME: 15 MINUTES

INGREDIENTS

250 g / 9 oz / 1 cup spinach leaves, washed

150 g / 5 oz / ⅔ cup mozzarella

4-6 floury potatoes, cooked and mashed (leftovers are perfect)

1 egg yolk

150 g / 5 oz / ⅔ cup plain (all-purpose) flour

pinch of paprika

olive oil

METHOD

1. Wilt the spinach leaves in a pan, then leave to cool. Drain as thoroughly as possible, then finely chop and set aside.
2. Drain the mozzarella then cut into small cubes.
3. Place the mashed potato in a bowl, then mix in the egg yolk, followed by the spinach and mozzarella. Season with salt and pepper.
4. Pat the mixture into small rounds or cakes. Mix the flour with a little seasoning and paprika, then dredge the cakes in it.
5. Heat about 1cm (½ in) depth of oil in a pan, then cook the cakes on both sides until crisp.
6. Drain on kitchen paper and serve hot.

Caponata stuffed aubergine

SERVES: 4 | PREP TIME: 20 MINUTES | COOKING TIME: 45 MINUTES

INGREDIENTS

2 aubergines (eggplants)
4 tbsp olive oil
1 onion, peeled and finely chopped
1 tsp dried oregano
2 cloves of garlic, peeled and finely sliced
2 celery stalks, chopped
bunch of flat-leaved parsley, chopped
2 tbsp capers, drained
12 green olives, stoned
3 tbsp red wine vinegar
4 ripe tomatoes, chopped
salt and pepper

METHOD

1. Preheat the oven to 200°C (180°C fan) / 400F / gas 6.
2. Cut the aubergines in half lengthways, drizzle with 2 tbsp oil and bake in the oven for about 30 minutes until tender.
3. Remove the flesh with a spoon, leaving the skin intact and with a margin of flesh to support the structure.
4. Heat the rest of the olive oil in the pan and cook the onion with oregano, garlic and celery until softened.
5. Add the aubergine and the rest of the ingredients and simmer for around 15 minutes until the vinegar has evaporated.
6. Season and spoon into the aubergine skins.
7. Serve immediately.

Pesto mozzarella arancini

SERVES: 4 | PREP TIME: 20 MINUTES | COOKING TIME: 10 MINUTES

INGREDIENTS

1 tbsp Parmesan, grated
4 tbsp pesto
1 ball mozzarella, cut into small cubes
275 g / 10 oz / 1 cup cooked Arborio rice, cold
1 tbsp plain (all-purpose) flour
1 egg, beaten
4 tbsp breadcrumbs
vegetable oil, for deep frying

METHOD

1. Stir the Parmesan, pesto and mozzarella through the risotto.
2. Shape into equal balls. If you prefer, you could make finger shapes instead. Lay out the flour, egg and breadcrumbs on separate plates.
3. Dip the risotto balls into the flour, then the egg, then the breadcrumbs. Use one hand and keep the other clean for ease.
4. Heat the oil to 180°C / 400F or until a cube of bread sizzles when dropped in the oil. Fry the risotto balls until golden and crisp all over.
5. Serve hot or warm.

Rocket Parmesan focaccia

SERVES: 4 | PREP TIME: 2 HOURS | COOKING TIME: 45 MINUTES

INGREDIENTS

FOR THE DOUGH

360 g / 12 ½ oz / 2 ⅓ cups '00' flour

¼ tsp salt

1 tsp fast-action dried yeast

75 ml / 3 fl. oz / ⅓ cup extra-virgin olive oil

250 ml / 9 fl. oz / 1 cup lukewarm water

FOR THE FILLING:

100 g / 4 oz / 1 ⅓ cups rocket (arugula) leaves

4 tbsp Parmesan cheese, grated

75 g / 3 oz / ⅔ cup pine kernels

black pepper

METHOD

1. Put the flour and salt into a bowl. Make a well. Add the yeast and 50 ml / 2 fl. oz olive oil and rub together. Pour in the water and mix until the dough comes together.
2. Tip the dough onto a floured surface and knead for 10 minutes until elastic. Place in an oiled bowl covered with film and leave for 1 ½ hours. Preheat the oven to 220°C (200°C fan) / 425 F / gas 7.
3. Uncover the dough and knead until smooth. Roll **two-thirds** into a circle about 30 cm wide and line a cake tin, lining the extra over the top.
4. Arrange the rocket leaves, Parmesan and pine kernels over the base. Drizzle with oil. Roll the remaining dough into a circle measuring about 25 cm. Lift onto the pie and press the edges together, sealing with water.
5. Trim the excess dough and brush with olive oil, then bake for 35 minutes.

Ricotta and spinach cake

SERVES: 6 | PREP TIME: 1 HOUR 20 MINUTES | COOKING TIME: 50 MINUTES

INGREDIENTS

500 g / 1 lb 2 oz / 4 ½ cups spinach, washed
1 clove garlic, crushed
40 g / 1 ½ oz / ⅓ stick butter
300 g / 10 ½ oz / 2 cups plain (all-purpose) flour
5 eggs
200 g / 7 oz / 1 ⅓ cups ricotta
150 g / 5 oz / 1 ½ cups Parmesan, grated
nutmeg, grated, to taste

METHOD

1. Wilt the spinach with the garlic in the butter. Season and cook until all the water has evaporated from the pan. Chop and set aside.
2. Place the flour, 3 eggs and a pinch of salt in the mixing bowl of a food processor and mix until they just come together to form a ball.
3. Remove from the bowl and work with your hands for 1 minute to make a smooth elastic dough. Wrap in film and leave in the refrigerator for 1 hour.
4. Roll out the pastry onto a floured surface, turning a quarter turn regularly to ensure you make a rectangle around 2 mm thick.
5. Mix the ricotta with the Parmesan, a pinch of salt and pepper and a little grated nutmeg, then whisk in 2 beaten eggs, followed by the spinach.
6. Spoon the mixture down one side of the pastry, then roll up to make a cylinder shape.
7. Wrap the entire cake in foil very tightly and securely and steam for about 45 minutes or until cooked. Allow to rest for 10 minutes before serving.

Italian appetisers

SERVES: 4 | PREP TIME: 30 MINUTES | COOKING TIME: 12 MINUTES

INGREDIENTS

1 sheet ready-rolled puff pastry
4 tbsp tapenade
8 sun-blushed tomato pieces
1 cucumber
4 tbsp mascarpone
3 tbsp pesto
1 tbsp pine nuts, lightly toasted
1 baguette or ciabatta
4 tbsp fruit chutney
4 slices Parma ham

METHOD

1. Preheat the oven to 200°C (180°C fan) / 400F / gas 6. Cut out eight circles from the puff pastry, 5 cm in diameter.
2. Place on a greased baking sheet and bake in the oven for about 12 minutes or until golden.
3. Remove from the oven and push down the centre of each circle to make a well in which to put the filling.
4. Once cool, spoon in a little tapenade and top with a sun-blushed tomato.
5. Run a vegetable peeler down the length of the cucumber to create an alternating striped effect. Cut the cucumber into rounds about 2 cm thick.
6. Mix together the mascarpone, pesto and pine nuts, then spoon a little onto each round of cucumber.
7. Slice the baguette into eight 2 ½cm (1 in) thick rounds and lightly toast under a grill.
8. Spoon a little fruit chutney on each one and top with a torn piece of Parma ham, folded into a rose shape.

Polenta and olive chips

SERVES: 4 | PREP TIME: 35 MINUTES | COOKING TIME: 55 MINUTES

INGREDIENTS

200 g / 7 oz / 1 cup polenta

1.5 l / 2 pints 12 fl. oz / 6 cups water

130 g / 4 ½ oz / 1 ¼ cups Parmesan, grated

2 handfuls black olives, stoned and chopped

oil for deep frying

METHOD

1. Whisk the polenta slowly into a large pan of boiling salted water.
2. As soon as it begins to boil, stir every 5 minutes, ensuring you push the spoon down into the sides of the pan.
3. Cook for about 45 minutes until it begins to have the consistency of mashed potato. Season and stir in the Parmesan and olives.
4. Oil a tray and tip the polenta out onto it. Spread the polenta to about 2.5 cm thick
5. Leave the polenta to cool for about 30 minutes, then cut into chip shapes when firm.
6. Heat the oil to 180°C / 400F. Deep-fry the polenta chips in batches until crisp.
7. Drain on kitchen paper and sprinkle with salt before serving.

Mini pizza appetisers

SERVES: 10 | PREP TIME: 45 MINUTES | COOKING TIME: 8-10 MINUTES

INGREDIENTS

FOR THE DOUGH

400 g / 14 oz / 2 ⅔ cups strong white bread flour
100 g / 3 ½ oz / ⅔ cup fine ground semolina flour
½ tbsp salt
1 x 7 g sachet dried yeast
½ tbsp caster (superfine) sugar
350 ml / 12 fl. oz / 1 ⅔ cup lukewarm water

FOR THE TOPPING:

6 tbsp bottled passata
handful of black olives, stoned
10 anchovies
small handful of rocket (arugula) leaves
2 tbsp pine kernels
basil, to garnish

METHOD

1. Pour the flour and salt into a bowl and make a well in the centre. Add the yeast and sugar to the water, mix with a fork and leave for 2 minutes. Pour into the well.
2. Bring in the flour from around the insides and mix into the water. When it starts coming together, use your hands and pat it into a ball.
3. Knead the dough for 10 minutes. Flour the dough, cover with film and leave for 30 minutes.
4. Preheat the oven to 240°C (220°C fan) / 475F / gas 9. Flour the surface, tear off a piece of dough and roll into a rough rectangle or square.
5. Dust each one with a little flour and lay out on the surface. Spread passata on each one, then top with olives, anchovies and rocket.
6. Sprinkle with pine kernels and place on a baking sheet. Bake for 8 minutes until golden.

Polenta galettes

SERVES: 4 | PREP TIME: 35 MINUTES | COOKING TIME: 45 MINUTES

INGREDIENTS

200 g / 7 oz / 1 cup polenta

1.5 litres / 2 pints 12 fl. oz / 6 cups water

130 g / 4 ½ oz / 1 ¼ cups Parmesan, grated

METHOD

1. Whisk the polenta slowly into a large pan of boiling salted water. As soon as it begins to boil, cover loosely with a lid and turn the heat down as low as possible.
2. Once it thickens, stir every 5 minutes, ensuring you push the spoon down into the sides of the pan.
3. Cook for about 45 minutes until it begins to have the consistency of mashed potato. Season generously and stir in the Parmesan.
4. Oil a tray and tip the polenta out onto to it. Spread the polenta to about 2.5 cm thick.
5. Leave the polenta to cool for about 30 minutes and then cut circles out 5 cm in diameter. Serve with your choice of topping.

Olive focaccia

SERVES: 2 | PREP TIME: 2 HOURS 40 MINUTES | COOKING TIME: 20 MINUTES

INGREDIENTS

750 g / 1 lb 10 oz / 5 cups '00' flour (Italian super-white flour)

½ tsp salt

2 tsp fast-action dried yeast

150 ml / 5 fl oz / ⅔ cup olive oil

450 ml / 16 fl. oz / 1 ⅔ cups lukewarm water

200 g / 7 oz / 1 ⅓ cups mixed olives, pitted and chopped

1 handful rosemary leaves

METHOD

1. Sift the flour and salt into a bowl. Make a well in the centre. Pour 2 tablespoons of the oil into the flour. Add the yeast. Rub together with your fingers. Pour in about 3/4 of the water and mix until the dough comes together. Tip the dough onto a floured surface. Knead for 10 minutes.
2. Place in an oiled bowl and cover with film. Leave to rise in a warm place for 1 hour 30 minutes.
3. Take the dough out and punch out the air. Work the olives into the dough. Divide into two balls. Roll into 2 circles. Place in two oiled pizza pans.
4. Cover with film and leave to rise for 30 minutes. Preheat the oven to 200°C (180°C fan) / 400F / gas 6. Uncover the dough and push your fingertips in to make deep dimples. Drizzle with oil so that the dimples fill up. Top with sprigs of rosemary.
5. Spray with water and bake for 20 minutes. Drizzle with oil. Transfer to a wire rack to cool, then serve.

Rosemary and olive focaccia

MAKES: 1 LOAF | PREP TIME: 20 MINUTES | COOKING TIME: 15 MINUTES

INGREDIENTS

345 g / 12 oz / 2 ⅓ cups plain (all-purpose) flour
1 tsp salt
1 tbsp dried active yeast
1 tsp dried oregano
1 tbsp rosemary, chopped
3 tbsp olive oil
235 ml / 8 fl. oz / ¾ cup water
25 g / 1 oz black olives, sliced

METHOD

1. In a large mixing bowl, combine the flour, salt, yeast, oregano and rosemary. Mix in 2 tablespoons of oil and the water.
2. Once the dough has formed, turn out onto a floured surface and knead until smooth and elastic. Lightly oil a large bowl and place the dough inside, cover with a damp cloth and leave in a warm place for 20 minutes until risen.
3. Preheat the oven to 220°C (200°C fan) / 425F / gas 7.
4. Turn out the dough onto a greased baking tray and form into a rough rectangle shape. Dot the chopped olives into the bread and brush with the remaining oil.
5. Bake in the oven for 15 minutes or until golden, remove from the oven and serve warm.

Focaccia pizza bread

MAKES: 1 LOAF | PREP TIME: 20 MINUTES | COOKING TIME: 15 MINUTES

INGREDIENTS

345 g / 12 oz / 2 ⅓ cups plain (all-purpose) flour
1 tsp salt
1 tbsp dried active yeast
1 tsp garlic granules
1 tsp dried oregano
1 tbsp rosemary, chopped
3 tbsp olive oil
235 ml / 8 fl. oz / ¾ cup water
25 g / 1 oz black olives, chopped
25 g / 1 oz tomatoes, chopped
50 g / 1 ¾ oz / ½ cup Parmesan cheese, grated

METHOD

1. In a large mixing bowl, combine the flour, salt, yeast, garlic, oregano and rosemary. Mix in 2 tablespoons of oil and the water.
2. Once the dough has formed, turn out onto a floured surface and knead until smooth and elastic. Lightly oil a large bowl and place the dough inside, cover with a damp cloth and leave in a warm place for 20 minutes until risen.
3. Preheat the oven to 220°C (200°C fan) / 425F / gas 7.
4. Turn out the dough onto a greased baking tray and form into a rough rectangle shape and brush with the remaining oil.
5. Sprinkle the surface with the chopped olives and tomatoes before topping with the grated cheese.
6. Bake in the oven for 15 minutes or until golden, remove from the oven and serve warm.

Smoked salmon crostini

MAKES: 20 | PREP TIME: 20 MINUTES | COOKING TIME: 10 MINUTES

INGREDIENTS

2 thin baguettes
50 ml / 1 ¾ fl. oz / ¼ cup olive oil
1 clove of garlic, minced
large bunch of fresh basil, leaves only
1 lemon, juice only
200 g / 7 oz / 1 cup cream cheese
400 g / 14 oz / 2 cups smoked salmon
20 caper berries

METHOD

1. To make the crostini bases, thinly slice the baguette. Brush with oil and place under a hot grill for 2-3 minutes on each side until crisp. Remove to cool and place into an airtight container until needed.
2. Place the remaining oil, garlic, basil and lemon into a blender and blend for a minute until combined.
3. To make the crostini, top the baguette slices with cream cheese followed by a slice of salmon. Drizzle with a small amount of the basil oil and finish with a caper berry.

Italian crisp breads

SERVES: 4 | PREP TIME: 15 MINUTES | COOKING TIME: 10MINUTES

INGREDIENTS

4 slices of wholemeal bread

50 g / 1 ¾ oz / ½ cup Parmesan cheese, grated

50 g / 1 ¾ oz mixed cherry tomatoes

1 avocado, peeled and sliced

2 tbsp extra virgin olive oil

1 lemon, juiced

100 g / 3 ½ oz / ½ cup ricotta cheese

25 g / 1 oz pine nuts

4 spring onions (scallions), sliced

METHOD

1. Preheat the oven to 180°C (160°C fan) / 350F / gas 4.
2. Toast the bread in a toaster until browned. Slice the bread lengthways into two halves so that one side is toasted and the other isn't.
3. Sprinkle the untoasted side with the Parmesan and place onto a baking tray. Bake in the oven for 10 minutes until the cheese has melted and the bread is crisp. Remove and cut each piece in half to make rectangles, then leave to cool.
4. In a bowl, mix the tomatoes, avocado, oil and lemon juice. Mix to combine and season with salt and black pepper.
5. When ready to serve spread each of the breads with the ricotta cheese before topping with the tomato and avocado mix. Sprinkle over the pine nuts and spring onions.

Ciabatta

MAKES: 2 LOAVES | PREP TIME: 2 HOURS | COOKING TIME: 25 MINUTES

INGREDIENTS

250 g / 9 oz / 1 ⅔ cup strong white bread flour

1 tsp salt

1 tsp active dried yeast

2 tbsp olive oil

200 ml / 7 fl. oz / ¾ cup water, at room temperature

1 tsp sugar

METHOD

1. Place the flour, salt and yeast into the bowl of a stand mixer with the bread hooks attached. Add the oil and half the water and mix. As it forms a dough, add the remaining water and sugar to the mixture and continue to mix for 10 minutes.
2. Place the dough into a lightly oiled rectangular container. Cover with a wet tea towel and leave to rise for 2 hours. It should have doubled or tripled in size by this time.
3. Preheat the oven to 220°C (200°C fan) / 425F / gas 7 and grease and line a baking tray.
4. Pour the dough out onto a floured surface. Mould into a rough rectangular shape. Cut into two strips and stretch out the dough lengthways to form a long sausage shape.
5. Place onto the baking tray and leave to rest for 15 minutes. Bake in the oven for 20-25 minutes until golden and hollow sounding when tapped on the base. Remove and allow to cool.

Avocado open sandwich

SERVES: 4 | PREP TIME: 15 MINUTES

INGREDIENTS

¼ crusty seeded bread

2 tbsp extra virgin olive oil

1 avocado

1 tbsp sunflower seeds

1 tbsp linseed

1 tsp flax seeds

sea salt and freshly ground black pepper

METHOD

1. Cut the bread in half lengthways and drizzle with the olive oil.
2. Cut the avocado in half and remove the stone. Remove the flesh with a spoon and cut into slices.
3. Place the sliced avocado on the bread and top with the mixed seeds.
4. Season with salt and black pepper and drizzle with additional oil as desired.

Cook's Corner
Irresistible Italian
Desserts

Panna cotta with berry jelly

SERVES: 4 | PREP TIME: 2-3 HOURS | COOKING TIME: 30 MINUTES

INGREDIENTS

4 gelatine leaves
200 ml / 7 fl. oz / ¾ cup milk
200 ml / 7 fl. oz / ¾ cup double (heavy) cream
1 vanilla pod, sliced lengthways seeds removed
50 g / 1 ¾ oz. / ¼ cup caster (superfine) sugar
200 g / 7 oz / 1 cup mixed berries, frozen
200 ml / 7 fl. oz / ¾ cup water
mint sprigs and fresh berries, to garnish

METHOD

1. Place the gelatine leaves into cold water to soak.
2. Place the milk, cream, vanilla pod and seeds, and half the sugar into a saucepan. Bring gradually up to a simmer. Remove the vanilla pod and discard.
3. Remove from the heat and add two gelatine leaves, stirring until dissolved. Leave to cool for a few minutes before pouring into ramekins or serving glasses. Place in the refrigerator for at least an hour to set.
4. For the jelly, add the remaining sugar, berries and water to a clean saucepan. Bring to a simmer until the berries start to break down and release their juice.
5. Strain into a clean saucepan and add the other two gelatine leaves. Place back onto the heat and stir to dissolve, then remove from the heat until cool.
6. Carefully pour the liquid jelly onto the set panna cotta, making sure the two don't mix.
7. Return to the fridge to set completely.
8. Serve garnished with fresh berries and mint sprigs.

Lemon granita

SERVES: 6-8 | PREP TIME: 15 MINUTES | FREEZING TIME: 4 HOURS

INGREDIENTS

200 g / 7 oz / ¾ cup caster (superfine) sugar
200 ml / 7 fl. oz / ¾ cup water
10 large lemons
150 ml / 5 fl. oz / ⅔ cup soda water

METHOD

1. Mix the sugar and water in a saucepan and heat enough to melt the sugar and create a syrup. Remove from the heat.
2. Zest the lemons into the warm syrup before juicing them and adding the juice to the mixture.
3. Stir in the soda water and pour into a sealable container that can be frozen.
4. Place in the freezer to start the freezing process. Remove every 45 minutes to an hour and break up with a fork so that ice crystals form. Continue to do this until all the liquid is frozen and you have an icy texture.
5. To serve, drag an ice cream scoop or strong spoon over the surface to break up the ice crystals.

Chocolate tiramisu

SERVES: 8 | PREP TIME: 30 MINUTES | COOKING TIME: 4 MINUTES

INGREDIENTS

500 g / 1 lb 2 oz / 2 cups mascarpone
150 g / 5 oz / ¾ cup caster (superfine) sugar
4 eggs, separated
200 g / 7 oz / 1 cup dark chocolate
250 ml / 8 fl. oz / 1 cup whole milk
2 tbsp rum (optional)
30 finger biscuits
cocoa powder, for dusting
8 chocolate squares

METHOD

1. Mix the mascarpone with the sugar and egg yolks until it forms a homogeneous cream.
2. Reserve half of the mixture.
3. Melt the chocolate over a bain-marie with half the milk and 1 tablespoon of rum, then leave to cool slightly. Add half the mascarpone mix.
4. Beat the egg whites until stiff and stir in half in the mascarpone cream and half in the chocolate mixture.
5. Add 1 tablespoon of rum to the remaining milk.
6. Dip the biscuits in this mixture and place half of them at the bottom of the individual serving dishes.
7. Cover with half the mascarpone cream, 2 tablespoons of the chocolate mix, and the rest of the mascarpone cream.
8. Carry on with the rest of the finger biscuits, the remaining chocolate mix and finish off with cocoa powder and a square of dark chocolate. Chill for up to 4 hours in the refrigerator before serving.

Vanilla and mint tiramisu

SERVES: 4 | PREP TIME: 2 HOURS

INGREDIENTS

1 cup strong black coffee, cooled
2 tbsp amaretto
2 eggs, separated
50 g / 1 ¾ oz / ¼ cup caster (superfine) sugar
125 g / 4 ¼ oz / ½ cup mascarpone
125 ml / 4 ½ fl. oz / ½ cup double (heavy) cream, whipped
1 tsp vanilla extract
2 tbsp crème de menthe
100 g / 3 ½ oz / ½ cup savoiardi biscuits
mint leaves, to garnish

METHOD

1. Mix the cooled coffee with the amaretto and set aside.
2. Whisk together the egg yolks and sugar until pale and creamy. Fold in the mascarpone and whipped cream to the egg mixture using a metal spoon.
3. Whisk the egg whites until soft peaks form. Fold into the mascarpone mixture along with the vanilla and crème de menthe, taking care not to lose any volume.
4. Break up the savoiardi biscuits and dip into the coffee mixture for a few seconds each.
5. Carefully layer the biscuits and cream mixture into four serving glasses, finishing with a layer of cream.
6. Place into the refrigerator for at least two hours or until firm, leave overnight for the best results. Garnish with a sprig of mint when ready to serve.

Amaretti

MAKES: 40 | PREP TIME: 30 MINUTES | COOKING TIME: 20 MINUTES

INGREDIENTS

1 egg white

1-2 tbsp almond extract

225 g / 8 oz / 2 cups ground almonds

150 g / 5 oz / 1 cup sifted icing (confectioner's) sugar

blanched almonds, to decorate (optional)

METHOD

1. Preheat the oven to 180°C (160°C fan) / 350 F / gas 4.
2. Grease 2 baking trays and cover with baking paper.
3. Whisk the egg white and almond extract in a bowl until frothy.
4. Put the ground almonds and icing sugar in a large bowl and make a well. Add the egg white and mix with a metal spoon until the dough is a soft texture.
5. Form into balls, about a teaspoon's worth of dough at a time, and arrange on the baking sheets, spacing them well. They can be decorated with a blanched almond each.
6. Cook the biscuits for 15-20 minutes. They should be lightly browned.
7. Let them cool on a rack.

Strawberry and mascarpone dessert

SERVES: 4 | PREP TIME: 35 MINUTES

INGREDIENTS

500 g / 1 lb 1 oz / 3 cups fresh strawberries
100 g / 3 ½ oz / ½ cup caster (superfine) sugar
50 g / 1 ¾ oz / ½ cup icing (confectioner's) sugar
100 ml / 3 ½ fl. oz / ½ cup double (heavy) cream
1 tsp vanilla essence
1 lemon, zest and juice
500 g / 1 lb 1 oz / 2 cups mascarpone
cocoa, to dust
mint sprigs, to garnish

METHOD

1. Dehull the strawberries. Separate off about a quarter and slice and place into a bowl with the caster sugar and cover. Leave for 30 minutes to macerate; they will be ready once the berries release their natural juices.
2. Place the remaining strawberries into a blender and blend to a pulp. Pass through a sieve into a clean bowl and mix with half the icing sugar to form a coulis.
3. Lightly whip the cream with the vanilla essence and lemon before stirring into the mascarpone. Add the juice from the macerated strawberries.
4. To make the dessert place alternate layers of mascarpone, strawberries and coulis into serving glasses. Top with a dusting of cocoa and garnish with sprigs of mint.

Bilberry tiramisu

SERVES: 4 | PREP TIME: 10 MINUTES | COOKING TIME: 3 HOURS

INGREDIENTS

200 g / 7 oz / 1 cup bilberries
60 g / 2 ½ oz / ½ cup brown sugar
a pinch cinnamon
250 g / 9 oz / 1 cup mascarpone
3 egg yolks
110 g / 4 oz / ½ cup caster (superfine) sugar
60 g / 2 ½ oz / ½ cup poppy seeds
1 tbsp of amaretto
120 ml / 4 fl. oz / ½ cup double (heavy) cream
4 madeleine cakes
4 tbsp Marsala wine

METHOD

1. Mix the bilberries with sugar and cinnamon. Cool and refrigerate for 1 hour.
2. In a bowl, whisk the mascarpone with the egg yolks, sugar, poppy seeds and amaretto.
3. Add the cream after whipping it until stiff. Cool and refrigerate.
4. Line the bottom of each glass with broken madeleine soaked in Marsala. Place a first layer of mascarpone cream, then the bilberries with cinnamon. Cover with a second layer of cream. Sprinkle with poppy seeds and cinnamon powder.
5. Cool and refrigerate for 2 hours before serving.

Sienna nougat with fruit

SERVES: 4 | PREP TIME: 10 MINUTES | COOKING TIME: 90 MINUTES
RESTING TIME: 10 MINUTES

INGREDIENTS

250 g / 9 oz / 1 cup liquid honey
350 g / 12 oz / 1 ¾ cup blanched almonds
200 g / 7 oz / 1 cup hazelnuts
225 g / 8 oz / 1 cup caster (superfine) sugar
3 egg whites
1 lemon and its zest
25 cl / 8 fl. oz / 1 cup double (heavy) cream
1 tbsp icing (confectioner's) sugar
100 g / 4 oz / ½ cup redcurrants
100 g / 4 oz / ½ cup raspberries
mint leaves, to garnish

METHOD

1. Place the honey in a bowl over a bain-marie and simmer for 10 minutes, stirring regularly.
2. Pre-heat the oven to 200°C (180°C fan) / 400F / gas 6. Grill the almonds and hazelnuts for 1 minute, checking to ensure they don't burn, then set aside.
3. In a pan, make a caramel with the sugar and 100ml / 3 fl. oz of water. Beat the egg whites until stiff then incorporate the honey mixture. Add the caramel. Mix for 5 minutes. Add the hazelnuts, almonds, lemon zest and juice. Pour the mixture on a rectangular tray lined with baking paper.
4. Level the mixture and cover with another baking paper. Cool for up to an hour then cut into small squares. The nougat can be kept in an airtight container.
5. To serve, beat the cream and add the icing sugar. Top the nougat squares with the cream, the washed redcurrants, raspberries and mint leaves.

Melon tiramisu

SERVES: 4 | PREP TIME: 10 MINUTES | COOKING TIME: 45 MINUTES

INGREDIENTS

1 cantaloupe melon

200 g / 7 oz / 1 cup fresh pineapple

350 ml / 12 fl. oz / 1 ½ cup double (heavy) cream

500 g / 1 lb 2 oz / 2 ½ cups mascarpone

150 g / 5 oz caster (superfine) sugar

120 ml / 4 fl. oz / ½ cup coconut milk

10 finger biscuits

1 tsp cinnamon powder, plus extra to serve

3 tbsp of grated coconut

METHOD

1. Cut the melon in four, remove the skin and seeds and cut into thin strips.
2. Cut the pineapple into very small dices.
3. Whip the cream until stiff, then add the mascarpone, sugar and coconut milk and whisk until the mixture is homogeneous.
4. Coarsely crush the finger biscuits, and arrange them in the bottom of a dish.
5. Sprinkle with coconut milk and a pinch of cinnamon.
6. Cover with half of the cream, then the melon and pineapple and the remaining cream.
7. Sprinkle with grated coconut and chill for at least 1 hour before serving.
8. Finish with cinnamon powder.

Fig and almond panetti

MAKES: 20 | PREP TIME: 10 MINUTES | COOKING TIME: 1 HOUR

INGREDIENTS

700 g / 1 lb 8 oz / 3 cups honey
400 g / 13 oz / 2 cups dark chocolate
50 g / 2 oz dried figs
200 g / 7 oz / 1 cup hazelnuts (cob nuts)
250 g / 9 oz / 1 cup almonds
450 g / 1 lb / 2 cups peanuts
700 g / 1 lb 8 oz / 3 cups plain (all-purpose) flour
120 ml / 4 fl. oz / ½ cup olive oil
2 tsp nutmeg, grated
1 tbsp black pepper
1 ½ tbsp cocoa powder

METHOD

1. Pour the honey into a pan with the chocolate cut into pieces.
2. Dissolve the honey and chocolate over low heat, stirring occasionally.
3. Cut the figs into small pieces, hazelnuts and almonds in half and leave the whole peanuts.
4. Put the flour in a bowl, pour the melted chocolate and honey and mix. Pour in the oil and mix again.
5. Add all the fruit and nuts, nutmeg, pepper and cocoa. Mix all the ingredients by hand.
6. Make dough balls and place them carefully on the baking sheet, spaced enough from each other. Rest for 10 hours if possible.
7. Cook the dough at 150°C (130°C fan) / 300F / gas 2 for about one hour, checking fairly frequently. Eat slightly warm.

Chocolate and chestnut tiramisu

SERVES: 4 | PREP TIME: 20 MINUTES | COOKING TIME: 1 HOUR

INGREDIENTS

150 g / 5 ¼ oz / ¾ cup whipped cream
250 g / 9 oz / 1 cup chestnut purée
200 g / 7 oz / 1 cup mascarpone
2 egg yolks
1 egg
35 g / 1 oz icing (confectioner's) sugar
6 finger biscuits
60 ml / 2 fl. oz / ¼ cup whisky
20 g / ¾ oz unsweetened cocoa
6 glazed chestnuts

METHOD

1. Whip the cream then gently fold in the chestnut purée.
2. Beat the mascarpone, 2 egg yolks and whole egg, then add the icing sugar.
3. Combine the two mixtures.
4. Soak the biscuits with the whisky, mixed with the cocoa.
5. Place the soaked crushed biscuits at the bottom of the serving dishes.
6. Top with the chestnut mixture.
7. Sprinkle with the glazed chestnuts.

Profiteroles

SERVES: 6 | PREP TIME: 45 MINUTES | COOKING TIME: 45 MINUTES

INGREDIENTS

FOR THE CHOUX PASTRY:

125 g / 4 ½ oz / ½ cup butter

1 tbsp sugar

2 pinches salt

150 g / 5 oz / 1 cup plain (all-purpose) flour

4 eggs

FOR THE SAUCE:

150 g / 5 oz / ½ cup dark chocolate

2 tbsp butter

1 tablespoon milk

FOR THE FILLING:

250 ml / 8 fl. oz / 1 cup double (heavy) cream

25 g / 1 oz icing (confectioner's) sugar

METHOD

1. Preheat the oven to 210°C (190°C fan) / 420 F / gas 7.
2. Heat the butter over low heat then add the sugar, salt and 250ml / 8 fl. oz / 1 cup of water and whisk.
3. Remove from the heat and add the flour. Whisk. Return to the heat and cook, stirring until the dough pulls away from pan.
4. Remove the pan from the heat. Stir in the eggs one at a time. Place the dough in a piping bag fitted with a plain tip. Form small balls of dough on a baking sheet. Space them out – they rise during cooking.
5. Bake for 30 minutes. Leave the oven door ajar to let the moisture escape.
6. Break the chocolate into a pan. Add the butter and milk. Melt over low heat, stirring until you obtain a sauce. Reserve in a water bath.
7. Beat the cream until stiff, then add the sugar and refrigerate. Remove the choux from the oven.
8. Cut the choux three-quarters of their height. Fill each with a small scoop of whipped cream. Place the caps on top. Place the choux in bowls and cover with chocolate sauce. Serve immediately.

Berry ice lollies

SERVES: 8 | PREP TIME: 15 MINUTES | FREEZING TIME: 4 HOURS

INGREDIENTS

200 g / 7 oz / ¾ cup silken tofu

200 ml / 7 fl. oz / ¾ cup coconut milk

1 lemon, juiced

100 g / 3 ½ oz / ½ cup caster (superfine) sugar

100 g / 3 ½ oz / ⅔ cup strawberries, hulled

100 g / 3 ½ oz / ⅔ cup blueberries

METHOD

1. Put the tofu, coconut milk, lemon juice and sugar in a liquidizer and blend until smooth.
2. Pour half of the mixture into an 8-hole ice lolly mould.
3. Add the strawberries to the rest of the mixture in the liquidizer and blend until smooth. Divide two thirds of the mixture between the lolly moulds.
4. Add the blueberries to the liquidizer and blend until smooth, then divide between the moulds. Add lolly sticks and freeze for 4 hours or until solid.

Strawberry gelato

SERVES: 6-8 | PREP TIME: 15 MINUTES | FREEZING TIME: 4 HOURS

INGREDIENTS

450 g / 1 lb / 2 ½ cups fresh strawberries

250 g / 9 oz / 1 ¼ cup caster (superfine) sugar

200 ml / 7 fl. oz / ¾ cup water

2 lemons, juiced

250 ml / 9 fl. oz / 1 cup double (heavy) cream

METHOD

1. Dehull the strawberries and cut in half. Add to a blender with the sugar, water and lemon juice. Blend until smooth and strain into a mixing bowl.
2. In a separate bowl, whisk the cream until thickened but not whipped.
3. Mix the strawberry mixture into the cream until combined.
4. Pour into an ice cream machine and process according to the manufacturer's instructions.
5. Place into the freezer for 4 hours or overnight to freeze completely.

Strawberry tiramisu

SERVES: 6 | PREP TIME: 30 MINUTES | CHILLING TIME: 3 HOURS

INGREDIENTS

6 egg yolks
125 g / 4 ½ oz / ½ cup of caster (superfine) sugar (100 g for mascarpone and 25 g for strawberries)
500 g / 1 lb 2 oz / 2 cups mascarpone
250 ml / 8 fl. oz / 1 cup whipping cream
350 g / 12 oz / 1 ½ cups strawberries
30 g / 1 oz pistachio paste
20 finger biscuits
120 ml / 4 fl. oz / ½ cup milk
crushed pistachios and mint leaves, for decoration

METHOD

1. Mix the egg yolks with 100 g / 3 ½ oz sugar until frothy.
2. Add the mascarpone and separate in 2 bowls.
3. Whip the cream until stiff. Add to the 2 mixtures. Blend half the strawberries with 25 g / 1 oz of sugar, then combine with one of the mascarpone mixtures. Combine the other mix with the pistachio paste.
4. Soak the finger biscuits in the milk and line the bottom of the serving dishes with half of them.
5. Top with the mascarpone mixture with pistachio, then half the remaining strawberries and the remaining biscuit.
6. Top with the strawberry mascarpone mixture and the rest of the strawberries, crushed pistachios and mint leaves. Chill for 3 hours.

Panna cotta with toffee

SERVES: 8 | PREP TIME: 20 MINUTES | RESTING TIME: 5 HOURS

INGREDIENTS

2 gelatine sheets
1 l / 2 pints / 4 cups whipping cream
110 g / 4 oz / ½ cup caster (superfine) sugar
1 vanilla pod

FOR THE TOFFEE SAUCE:
120 g / 4 oz / ½ cup butter
110 g / 4 oz / ½ cup light brown sugar
90 ml / 3 fl. oz / ⅓ cup double (heavy) cream

FOR THE ALMOND BRITTLE:
450 g / 1 lb / 2 cups caster (superfine) sugar
120 ml / 4 fl. oz / ½ cup water
pinch of salt
200 g / 7 oz / 2 cups flaked (silvered) almonds

METHOD

1. Soak the gelatine sheets in cold water. Drain them and reserve. Boil the cream with the sugar and vanilla pod cut lengthways.
2. Turn off the heat and add the gelatine, stirring. Strain the cream then let it cool, stirring often. Pour the cream into serving glasses and keep in fridge for 5 to 6 hours.
3. Meanwhile, prepare the toffee sauce by melting the butter and sugar in a saucepan over low heat until the sugar dissolves (without burning).
4. Stir in the cream gently until boiling, then stir and let cool before pouring on top of the set panna cotta.
5. To prepare the almond brittle stir together the sugar, water and salt in a saucepan and cook over medium heat until golden brown then remove from the heat and stir in the almonds.
6. Pour the mixture on a baking tray, then allow to cool for about 15 minutes before breaking into pieces.

Mascarpone ice cream with berries

SERVES: 6 | PREP TIME: 20 MINUTES | FREEZING TIME: 6 HOURS

INGREDIENTS

250 ml / 8 fl. oz / 1 cup double (heavy) cream
400 g / 13 oz / 2 cups mascarpone
250 ml / 8 fl. oz / 1 cup cane sugar syrup
mixed berries, to serve

METHOD

1. In a bowl, whip the cream until stiff, but not churned.
2. In a separate bowl, whisk the mascarpone with the sugar cane syrup.
3. Fold the whipped cream into the mascarpone and sugar mixture.
4. Pour the mixture into a silicone cake mould and cover with plastic wrap. Press down well and freeze for at least 6 hours.
5. When ready to serve, unmould or use an ice cream scoop to serve the ice cream. Serve with mixed berries in a dessert glass.

Zuppa inglese

SERVES: 4 | PREP TIME: 15 MINUTES | COOKING TIME: 10-14 MINUTES

INGREDIENTS

500 ml / 1 pt / 2 cups whole milk
100 g / 4 oz / ¾ cup caster (superfine) sugar
125 g / 4 ½ oz / ¾ cup dark chocolate
75 g / 3 oz cornstarch
250 g / 9 oz plain panettone or brioche
4 eggs
1 tsp of instant coffee

METHOD

1. Heat three-quarters of the milk with one-quarter of the sugar and the chocolate until completely melted, then incorporate the cornstarch and cook until the mixture thickens.
2. Let the mixture cool, stirring occasionally, then incorporate the coffee and stir.
3. Pre-heat the oven to 180°C (160°C fan) / 350F / gas 4. Meanwhile, cut the brioche and soak it in a mix of the remaining milk, 1 egg and 3 egg yolks.
4. Place half the soaked brioche in the bottom of a buttered dish, then top with the chocolate / coffee cream, then with the rest of the brioche.
5. Cook for 15 minutes, until the brioche firms up. Meanwhile, beat the remaining 3 egg whites until stiff, then add the remaining sugar. Beat again until the sugar is dissolved.
6. Let the cake cool down, then cover with the egg white mixture and place in the oven for 5 minutes under the grill. The meringue should just start to brown. Allow to cool slightly before serving.

Raspberry tiramisu

SERVES: 6 | PREP TIME: 20 MINUTES | COOKING TIME: 2 HOURS

INGREDIENTS

500 g / 1 lb 2 / 2 ½cups mascarpone

110 g / 4 oz / ½ cup caster (superfine) sugar

2 eggs, separated

250 g / 9 oz / 1 ¼ cup raspberries

12 finger biscuits

150 ml / 5 fl. oz / ½ cup Marsala

cocoa powder, to serve

METHOD

1. Mix the mascarpone with the sugar and beaten eggs yolks.
2. Whisk the egg whites to soft peaks and fold into the egg yolk mixture.
3. Purée the raspberries, keeping a few for decoration.
4. Place the raspberry coulis at the bottom of the serving dishes.
5. Dip the finger biscuits in Marsala. Place them over the raspberry coulis. Add the mascarpone mixture then dust with cocoa powder. Finish with the fresh raspberries and chill for 2 hours.

Chocolate ice cream

SERVES: 6 | PREP TIME: 1 HOUR | COOKING TIME: 20 MINUTES

INGREDIENTS

250 g / 9 fl. oz / 1 cup evaporated milk

250 ml / 9 fl. oz / 1 cup milk

4 tbsp caster (superfine) sugar

3 egg yolks

150 g / 5 oz / ½ cup dark chocolate

150 g / 5 oz / ¾ cup full-fat plain yogurt

METHOD

1. Mix the evaporated milk with the milk in a saucepan and heat without boiling.
2. Mix the sugar and egg yolks and pour the mixture gently into the hot milk mixture, stirring constantly. Cook for 10 minutes.
3. Melt the chocolate over a bain-marie then slowly incorporate the chocolate to the milk.
4. Remove from the heat and let cool to room temperature. Add the yogurt and mix well, then refrigerate.
5. Churn for 40 minutes in an ice cream maker or place in the freezer for 4 hours, whisking regularly until frozen.

Raspberry tiramisu sorbet

SERVES: 6 | PREP TIME: 4 HOURS 20 MINUTES | COOKING TIME: 10 MINUTES

INGREDIENTS

150 ml / 5 fl. oz / ⅔ cup Marsala
400 g / 14 oz / 2 cups mascarpone
4 tbsp crème fraîche
120 g / 5 oz / ⅔ cup icing (confectioner's) sugar
400 g / 14 oz / 2 cups raspberries
12 finger biscuits
500 ml / 1 pt / raspberry sorbet
6 mint leaves, for decoration

METHOD

1. Boil **two-thirds** of the Marsala with 200ml / 7 fl. oz of water. Cool and filter.
2. Whisk the mascarpone in a bowl with the crème fraîche, half the icing sugar and remaining Marsala.
3. Mash half the raspberries with the remaining sugar then filter to get rid of the pips and get a smooth raspberry coulis.
4. Dip the finger biscuits into the Marsala mixture. Place half the mascarpone mixture in the serving dishes, then the finger biscuits and half the raspberry coulis.
5. Top with the rest of the mascarpone cream and the rest of the coulis. Sprinkle with the remaining raspberries. Put the tiramisu in the fridge for at least 4 hours.
6. Serve chilled with a scoop of raspberry sorbet and some mint leaves.

Mini orange ciambellone

SERVES: 8 | PREP TIME: 20 MINUTES | COOKING TIME: 30 MINUTES

INGREDIENTS

200 g / 7 oz / 1 cup unsalted butter
300 g / 10 ½ oz / 1 ⅓ cup caster (superfine) sugar
4 free-range eggs, separated
300 g / 10 ½ oz / 2 cups plain (all-purpose) flour
100 g / 3 ½ oz / ⅔ cup cornflour (cornstarch)
1 orange, zest only
25 ml / 1 fl. oz milk
1 tsp baking powder
½ tsp vanilla essence
icing (confectioner's) sugar to dust

METHOD

1. Preheat the oven to 160°C (140°C fan) / 325F / gas 3. Grease 8 mini bundt cake moulds.
2. Place the butter and all but one tablespoon of sugar into the bowl of a mixer and mix.
3. Stir in the egg yolks, flours, orange zest and a splash of milk. Mix until soft peaks form.
4. Add the baking powder and vanilla essence to the mixture and mix through.
5. Whisk the egg whites with the remaining tablespoon of sugar until soft peaks form. Fold this into the cake mixture.
6. Spoon the mixture into the prepared moulds and bake in the oven for 20 minutes. They should be golden and springy to the touch.
7. Turn out of the moulds to cool and dust with icing sugar when ready to serve.

Raspberry panna cotta

SERVES: 8 | PREP TIME: 5 HOURS 20 MINUTES | COOKING TIME: 10 MINUTES

INGREDIENTS

3 gelatine sheets
1 l / 2 pts / 4 cups whipping cream
110 g / 4 oz / ½ cup sugar
1 vanilla pod
500 g / 1 lb 2 oz / 2 cups raspberries
200 g / 7 oz / 1 cup sugar
8 mint leaves, for decoration

METHOD

1. Soak the gelatine in cold water, drain and reserve.
2. Boil the cream with the sugar and vanilla pod cut in its length. Turn off the heat and add the gelatine, stirring.
3. Strain the cream and let it cool, stirring often. Pour the cream into the serving dishes and keep in the fridge for 5 hours.
4. Prepare a coulis by mixing the cleaned raspberries (minus a handful for decoration) and the sugar. Keep in the fridge.
5. Before serving, unmould the panna cotta or serve it in its glass with the raspberry coulis and fresh raspberries and mint leaves.

Gingerbread and orange tiramisu

SERVES: 6 | PREP TIME: 15 MINUTES | COOKING TIME: 1 HOUR

INGREDIENTS

300 g / 10 ½ oz / 2 cups plain flour
1 ½ tsp ground ginger
160 g / 5 ½ oz / 1 ½ sticks butter
75 g / 3 oz / ⅓ cup golden caster sugar
125 g / 4 ½ oz / ½ cup honey
110 g / 4 oz / ⅓ cup golden syrup
1 large egg
175 ml / 6 fl. oz / ¾ cup milk
250 ml / 9 fl. oz / 1 cup cold water
225 g / 8 oz / 1 cup caster sugar
1 orange, juiced and zested
500 ml / 1 pint / 2 cups whipping cream
250 g / 9 oz / 1 cup mascarpone
75 ml / 3 fl. oz / ⅓ cup Marsala
75 g / 3 oz / ⅓ cup golden caster sugar

METHOD

1. Preheat the oven to 180°C (160°C fan) / 350F / gas 4.
2. Grease a tin and line with greaseproof paper. Sift together the flour and ground ginger.
3. Whisk the butter and sugar until fluffy. Beat in the honey and golden syrup and mix 2 tbsp of the flour mixture and beat the egg in.
4. Fold in the flour, then follow with the milk. Spoon into the tin and bake for 45 minutes.
5. Combine the water and sugar in a pan and cook over a low heat. Simmer for 5 minutes before adding the orange juice and zest and cook for 10 minutes.
6. Remove the gingerbread and let it cool, then slice into triangles. Pour over the orange mixture.
7. Combine the cream, mascarpone, Marsala and sugar in a bowl and whisk. Spread the cream into the base of a glass dish. Arrange the triangles on top. Sprinkle the top with the cocoa powder.

Lemon polenta flan

SERVES: 6 | PREP TIME: 20 MINUTES | COOKING TIME: 30 MINUTES

INGREDIENTS

250 ml / 8 fl. oz / 1 cup cream
500 ml / 1 pt / 2 cups milk
150 g / 5 oz / ⅔ cup sugar
125 ml / 4 fl. oz / ½cup water
1 lemon
125 g / 4 ½ oz / ¾ cup polenta
1 vanilla pod
4 eggs

METHOD

1. Pre-heat the oven to 180°C (160°C fan) / 350F / gas 4.
2. Mix the cream, milk, sugar, water, lemon juice and zest, polenta, vanilla pod and eggs together. Whisk to obtain a consistent cream.
3. Heat on medium heat, stirring constantly with a whisk. After about 10 minutes, it should thicken. Turn off the heat and pour the mixture into a buttered flan tin.
4. Cook for 25 minutes in the oven and cool in the refrigerator for 2 hours.
5. Serve cold or slightly warmed.

Polenta sage madeleines

SERVES: 4 | PREP TIME: 15 MINUTES | COOKING TIME: 20 MINUTES

INGREDIENTS

handful sage leaves, finely sliced

2 eggs

80 g / 3 oz / ⅓ cup caster (superfine) sugar

100 g / 4 oz / ½ cup plain (all-purpose) flour

1 tsp baking powder

150 ml / 5 fl. oz / ⅔ cup olive oil

2 tbsp polenta

1 lemon, juiced

METHOD

1. Preheat the oven to 200°C (180°C fan) / 400F / gas 6.
2. Oil a madeleine mould tray and line a sage leave at the bottom of each madeleine shape.
3. In a bowl, beat the eggs. Still beating, add the sugar, flour and baking powder.
4. Stir in olive oil and the thinly sliced sage and carry on beating. Finish by adding the polenta and lemon juice.
5. Once the mixture is smooth, fill the moulds with the batter and bake for 15-20 minutes. Check they are cooked with a knife point.
6. Serve the madeleines with jam or grated coconut and chocolate sauce.

Pipasena Italian cake

SERVES: 6 | PREP TIME: 20 MINUTES | COOKING TIME: 40 MINUTES

INGREDIENTS

125 g / 4 ½ oz / ¾ cup raisins
125 g / 4 ½ oz / ¾ cup candied fruits
2 tbsp dark rum
1 lemon
225 ml / 8 fl. oz / 1 cup milk
125 g / 4 ½ oz / ¾ cup butter
450 g / 1 lb / 3 ½ cups plain (all-purpose) flour
1 tsp baking powder
2 eggs
200 g / 7 oz / 1 cup sugar
1 sachet vanilla sugar
3 tbsp oil

METHOD

1. Pre-heat the oven to 190°C (170°C fan) / 375F / gas 5.
2. Mix the raisins, candied fruits, rum and a little water in a bowl to marinate them.
3. Heat in the microwave oven for 1 minute and let cool.
4. Grate the zest of lemon.
5. Heat the milk and butter until the butter is melted. Mix the flour and baking powder, then add the eggs and the milk mixture.
6. Add the sugar, vanilla sugar and oil. Fold in the grated zest and drained fruits and raisins gently.
7. Cook for 40 minutes.

Cappuccino cream dessert

SERVES: 8 | PREP AND RESTING TIME: 45 MINUTES | COOKING TIME: 15 MINUTES

INGREDIENTS

50 g / 2 oz cornstarch
125 g / 4 ½ oz / ¾ cup caster (superfine) sugar
25 g / 1 oz unsweetened bitter cocoa
50 g / 2 oz cappuccino powder mix
1 litre / 2 pts / 4 cups milk
30 cl / 10 fl. oz liquid whipping cream
1 tbsp icing (confectioner's) sugar
chocolate sauce

METHOD

1. Mix the cornstarch, sugar, unsweetened cocoa mixture and cappuccino with cold milk.
2. Bring to a boil in a heavy saucepan and let thicken, stirring constantly to prevent burning.
3. Once the desired consistency is reached (usually just before boiling), remove from the heat and add half the cream.
4. Leave to cool at room temperature for about 30 minutes, stirring occasionally.
5. Meanwhile, whisk the rest of the cream until stiff then add the icing sugar and whisk more.
6. Place the cream in cups, and top with chantilly cream with a piping bag and a sprinkle of chocolate sauce.

Ricotta cake

SERVES: 4 | PREP TIME: 15 MINUTES | COOKING TIME: 50 MINUTES

INGREDIENTS

250 g / 9 oz / 1 ¼ cup ricotta

3 eggs

150 g / 5 oz / ¾ cup caster (superfine) sugar

pinch powdered ginger

1 lemon, grated zest and juiced

60 ml / 2 fl. oz / ¼ cup milk

150 g / 5 oz / ¾ cup plain (all-purpose) flour

METHOD

1. Pre-heat the oven to 200°C (180°C fan) / 400F / gas 6.
2. Put in the bowl the ricotta, eggs, sugar and ginger, then whip until smooth.
3. Add the grated lemon zest and juice, beat again, then add the milk.
4. Add the flour gradually.
5. Pour the batter into a buttered and floured pan.
6. Cook in the oven for 30 to 40 minutes. When cooked, the cake should be puffed and golden.
7. Serve warm or cold.

Strawberry zabaglione

SERVES: 6 | PREP TIME: 40 MINUTES | COOKING TIME: 5 MINUTES

INGREDIENTS

500 g / 1 lb / 2 cups strawberries

1 lemon

150 g / 5 oz / caster (superfine) sugar

250 ml / 8 fl. oz / 1 cup water

2 tbsp white balsamic vinegar

1 tsp cardamom seeds

100 g / 4 oz / ½ cup honey

3 eggs

100 ml / 3 ½ oz / ½ cup double (heavy) cream

125 g / 4 ½ oz / ½ cup mascarpone

6 mint leaves

METHOD

1. Wash and hull the strawberries and cut them in two. Mix them with the juice of half the lemon and a tablespoon of caster sugar and reserve.
2. Boil half the remaining sugar, water, vinegar and half the cardamom seeds to make a syrup.
3. In another saucepan, caramelize the honey with the remaining cardamom and zest of lemon.
4. Mix the flavoured honey with the syrup, then refrigerate. After cooling, filter and sprinkle half the strawberries and marinate for 20 minutes. Reserve.
5. Break the eggs, add the remaining sugar and beat until white and compact. Beat the cream until stiff, mix with the cheese and add to the previous mixture.
6. Arrange the fruit in syrup at the bottom of the serving dishes and top with the mascarpone cream. Finish with the remaining strawberries and fresh mint leaves for serving.

Panforte di Sienna

SERVES: 8 | PREP TIME: 15 MINUTES | COOKING TIME: 40 MINUTES

INGREDIENTS

100 g / 4 oz / ½ cup candied fruit peel (oranges or lemons)
75 g / 3 oz blanched hazelnuts (cob nuts)
75 g / 3 oz blanched almonds
50 g / 2 oz plain (all-purpose) flour
50 g / 2 oz cocoa powder
¼ tsp allspice powder
¼ tsp ground cinnamon
100 g / 4 oz / ½ cup liquid honey
100 g / 4 oz / ½ cup caster (superfine) sugar
icing (confectioner's) sugar, to decorate

METHOD

1. Preheat the oven to 160°C (140°C fan) / 315F / gas 3.
2. Finely chop the fruit. Mix with the hazelnuts and almonds. Mix everything in a bowl with the flour, cocoa, allspice and cinnamon.
3. Prepare a syrup: pour the honey and sugar in a pan. Heat over low heat until the sugar dissolves. Bring to a boil. Stir until the mix forms a ball.
4. Remove from the heat and pour into the bowl, and combine everything.
5. Line a cake pan with a sheet of baking paper and smooth the dough to 2cm (1 in) thick. Place in the oven and bake for 30 to 35 minutes.
6. When the cake is golden brown, let it cool. Just before serving, dust with icing sugar.

Rhubarb tiramisu

SERVES: 4 | PREP TIME: 4 HOURS 15 MINUTES | COOKING TIME: 15 MINUTES

INGREDIENTS

FOR THE MASCARPONE CREAM:

1 egg, separated

100 g / 4 oz caster (superfine) sugar

200 g / 7 oz / 1 cup mascarpone

FOR THE RHUBARB COMPOTE:

5 large stalks rhubarb

110 g / 4 oz brown sugar

FOR THE BASE:

200 g cinnamon finger biscuits

110 g / 4 oz / 1 stick butter

METHOD

1. To prepare the mascarpone cream, mix the egg yolk, sugar and mascarpone and stir in the egg white, after beating it until stiff. Then chill.
2. Wash and chop the rhubarb stalks. Cook them with the sugar in a covered pan over low heat, stirring with a wooden spoon. Reserve.
3. To prepare the base, blend 150 g / 5 oz cinnamon biscuits. Combine it with the softened butter.
4. Place the biscuit base in serving dishes, then half the mascarpone cream and the rhubarb compote. Crumble a couple of biscuits on top of the rhubarb, then the rest of the mascarpone cream.
5. Chill in the fridge for at least 4 hours. Just before serving, the dishes can be sprinkled with cocoa powder, crumbled biscuits or a pinch of cinnamon powder.

Polenta chocolate cookies

SERVES: 10 | PREP TIME: 15 MINUTES | COOKING TIME: 15 MINUTES

INGREDIENTS

1 egg
3 tsp brown sugar
3 tsp butter
2 tbsp instant polenta
2 tbsp plain (all-purpose) flour
½ tsp baking powder
2 tbsp chocolate chips

METHOD

1. Preheat the oven to 180°C (160°C fan) / 350F / gas 4.
2. In a bowl, whisk the egg with the sugar then add the butter and mix well.
3. Add the polenta (without cooking it before), flour and baking powder.
4. Once the mixture is smooth, take a tablespoon of dough, quickly forming a ball with your fingers and place on a baking sheet. Flatten with a spoon to form the cookie.
5. Space the cookies well on the sheet. Cook for 15 minutes, then add the chocolate chips (they should stick to the cookies but not melt).
6. Remove from the oven and transfer to a wire rack to cool.

Champagne zabaglione

SERVES: 4 | PREP TIME: 15 MINUTES | COOKING TIME: 10-14 MINUTES

INGREDIENTS

8 egg yolks

180 g / 6 oz / caster (superfine) sugar

1 tsp vanilla extract

1 lemon, grated zest and juiced

400 ml / 13 fl. oz / 2 cups Champagne

200 g / 7 oz / ¾ cup raspberries

METHOD

1. Put the egg yolks in a saucepan. Place the saucepan over a water bath, on a medium heat.
2. Add the sugar, vanilla and lemon zest. Whisk until foamy and pale.
3. Put the saucepan into a water bath on medium heat, then stir in the Champagne gradually while beating.
4. Purée the raspberries and filter to remove the pips. Add to the mixture and fold gently.
5. Serve the warm zabaglione with almond biscuits or gingerbread.

Strawberry and melon lollies

SERVES: 6-8 | PREP TIME: 10 MINUTES | FREEZING TIME: 4 HOURS

INGREDIENTS

½ watermelon

400 g / 14 oz / 2 cups strawberries, fresh or frozen

handful of fresh mint, chopped

1 lime, juiced

METHOD

1. Peel the watermelon and cut into cubes, removing the seeds as you go.
2. If using fresh strawberries dehull and chop into halves.
3. Add the ingredients to a blender and blend for a couple of minutes, according to the manufacturer's instructions, until smooth.
4. Pour into lolly moulds and place into the freezer for at least 4 hours or ideally overnight. They will be ready once completely frozen.

Mascarpone ice cream

SERVES: 46 | PREP TIME: 15 MINUTES | COOKING TIME: 15 MINUTES
FREEZING TIME: 4 HOURS

INGREDIENTS

2 large free-range egg yolks

75 g / 2 ½ oz / ⅓ cup caster (superfine) sugar

200 ml / 7 fl. oz / ¾ cup full fat milk

200 g / 7 oz / 1 cup mascarpone cheese

1 tsp vanilla essence

ice cream waffles, cherry jam (jelly) and chopped pistachio nuts, to serve

METHOD

1. Whisk together the egg yolks and sugar until pale and creamy. Heat the milk, mascarpone and vanilla in a saucepan. Whisk continuously until just about boiling.
2. Pour the hot milk mixture into the eggs and sugar. Whisk constantly while doing this stop it from becoming lumpy. This will form a custard.
3. Clean the saucepan and pour the custard into this. Gradually heat stirring constantly until it has thickened enough to coat the back of a spoon, take care not to let this boil.
4. Sieve the mixture into a clean bowl, and once cooled, process in an ice cream machine. Once churned, place into the freezer for 4 hours or overnight to completely freeze.
5. To serve, place a scoop of ice cream into an ice cream waffle cup and top with a spoonful of cherry jam and chopped pistachio nuts.

Orange cake with amaretto caramel

SERVES: 8-10 | PREP TIME: 20 MINUTES | COOKING TIME: 3 HOURS

INGREDIENTS

2 oranges
6 free-range eggs
250 g / 9 oz / 2 ½ cups ground almonds
250 g / 9 oz / 1 ¼ cup caster (superfine) sugar
1 tbsp baking powder
100 g / 3 ½ oz / ½ cup soft brown sugar
100 ml / 3 ½ fl. oz / ½ cup double (heavy) cream
1 tbsp salted butter
2 tbsp amaretto

METHOD

1. Thoroughly wash the oranges and place into a saucepan filled with simmering water. Cook for 2 hours until softened.
2. Drain the oranges and then set aside to cool. Cut into quarters, peel away the skin and remove the pips. Place the remaining flesh into a blender and blend to a pulp.
3. Preheat the oven to 180°C (160°C fan) / 350F / gas 4 and grease and line a 20cm cake tin.
4. Beat the eggs and add the almonds, sugar and baking powder. Mix into a batter and stir in the orange pulp until fully combined.
5. Pour into the prepared cake tin and bake for around an hour until golden and a skewer inserted into the centre of the cake comes out clean.
6. To make the caramel sauce, combine the brown sugar, cream and butter in a saucepan. Bring to the boil before reducing the heat and leaving to simmer for around 10 minutes. Stir very occasionally, then remove from the heat and stir through the amaretto.
7. Serve slices of the cake with a drizzle of caramel sauce.

INDEX